THE ULTIMATE DESSERT COOKBOOK

AARAV M HO

Copyright © 2023 Aarav M Ho

All rights reserved.

CONTENTS

MAKING VINTAGE PIE 1

A Bit of History

Tips for Making the Perfect Pie

CUSTARD PIES 10

Egg Custard Pie

Old-Fashioned Buttermilk Pie

Flapper Pie

Chess Pie

Tyler Pie

Vinegar Pie

Cream Pie

Boston Cream Pie

CHOCOLATE PIES 23

Chocolate Custard Pie

Chocolate Fudge Pie

Chocolate Chip Pie

Chocolate Rum Pie

Chocolate Black Bottom Pie

Frozen Mud Pie

Banoffee Pie

Possum Pie

Whoopie Pies

Cocoa Cream Pie

Marshmallow and Chocolate Pie

SUGAR AND OTHER SWEET PIES 44

Sugar Cream Pie

Indiana Sugar Cream Pie

Maple Syrup Pie

Butterscotch Pie

Burnt Caramel Pie

Jefferson Davis Pie

Oatmeal Pie

Mock Apple Pie

SPECIAL OCCASION PIES 59

Mincemeat Pie

Pumpkin Pie

No-Bake Pumpkin Pie

Pumpkin Chiffon Pie

Easy Streusel Pumpkin Pie

Italian Easter Pie

Fruit Cocktail Eggnog Pie

Eggnog Chiffon Pie

Funeral Pie

Marlborough Pie

Soda Cracker Pie

NUT AND DRIED 80
FRUIT-BASED PIES 80

Mom's Pecan Pie

Old-Fashioned Pecan Pie

Caramel Pecan Pie

Bourbon Pecan Pie

Kentucky Derby Pie

Praline Pie

Bakewell Tart

Raisin Pie

Kool Aid Pie

Hillbilly Pie

Shoofly Pie

APPLE-BASED PIES **98**

Apple Cheddar Pie

Apple Scottish Pie

Apple Crumble Pie

Norwegian Apple Pie

Johnny Appleseed Pie

King Kamehameha Pie

Candy Apple Pie

Apple Butter Hand Pies

BERRY PIES **115**

Blueberry Pie

Maine's Settler Blueberry Pie

Creamy Blue Pie

Cherry Pie

Impossible Cherry Pie

Royal Cranberry Pie

Old-Fashioned Gooseberry Pie

Curly Slab Jam Pie

Mom's Strawberry Pie

Easy Peasy No-Bake Strawberry Pie

Strawberry Sponge Pie

Jell-O™ Strawberry Pie

Crumbled Strawberry Pie

CITRUSY PIES **137**

Lemon Cream Pie

Lemon Meringue Pie

Lemon Whey Pie

No-Bake Whipped Angel Food Pie

Angel Pie

Lemonade Chiffon Pie

Lemonade Icebox Pie

Lime Cheesecake Pie

COCONUT AND PINEAPPLE PIES 152

Pineapple Cream Pie

Pineapple No-Bake Pie

Millionaire Pie

Frozen Tropical Pie

Sawdust Pie

Coconut Pie

Koko Nut Pie

OTHER FRUITY PIES 161

Apricot Icebox Pie

Banana Rum Pie

Banana Cream Pie

Cherry-Peach Pandowdy

Peach Pie

Peach Parfait Pie

Old-Fashioned Pear Pie

Rhubarb Strawberry Pie

Mom's Vintage Rhubarb Pie

MAKING VINTAGE PIE

There's nothing like the scent of freshly baked pie in the kitchen, but the days when baking a homemade pie signaled a special occasion are gone. Many of us look back on that tradition with fondness, remembering those pies as the number one comfort food. Those were the days when mom or grandma had painstakingly prepared a special pie packed with love and deliciousness.

It's easy to get a piece of the pie nowadays. You can get it pre-baked from your convenience store, or at your local pastry shop or café. There are pre-made fillings and crusts. It's never been this easy.

But those who have baked pies from scratch know the rewarding joy that comes with making one. Some say there is something almost spiritual about baking pies. Every bite of homemade pie seems to impart the maker's love and devotion. This is perhaps why old-fashioned, home-baked pies come with so many warm, fuzzy feelings and memories.

Baking old-fashioned pies may be becoming a lost art. This is such a pity, as these traditional pies are packed, not only with luscious flavors but with history and a testament to the persistence and optimism of the pie-makers – our mothers and grandmothers – during times of difficulty. Indeed, recession and war gave birth to such amazing vintage pies as Mock Apple Pie, Vinegar Pie, and Sugar Pie. To forget these pies, which are so much a part of our history, would be a loss to our culture and heritage.

This cookbook will bring you back to those times when pies were made out of devotion and persistence, proving our love for family and good things, our creativity, and our victory over hardship and limitation.

A Bit of History

Ancient Egypt and Greece are where pies first appeared. The ancient Greeks consumed pie (artocreas), but it was savory and had meat inside an exposed pastry crust. It's possible that the first people to create a pie with a top and bottom crust were the Romans. One of the earliest records of a closed pie is the placenta (flat cake) recipe from Marcus Porcius Cato (Cato the Elder)'s *Agri Cultura* from the second century (BCE). According to several interpretations, it was made by enclosing a sweet, dense filling of goat cheese, honey, and layers of pastry dough (tracta) with a bottom and top crust.

The people of 16th-century England are frequently credited with the rise in popularity of the sweet fruit pie or tart. Cherry pie was a favorite food of Elizabeth I, and there are fruit pie recipes in the *Newe Booke of Cokerye* (1575) A number of recipes for fruit and meat crostate (pie/tarts) are also included in Bartolomeo Scappi's *Opera* (1570).

Royalty and the higher class would commission their chefs to create gorgeous pies using living animals in order to dazzle guests. A later example of a recipe that contained both live birds and frogs is the *Accomplish Cook's* (1671) Live Birds in a Pie recipe.

By the 17th century, sweet pies and tarts had become more common. The 1694 book *The Compleat Cook: or, the Whole Art of Cookery* has a chapter on "Tarts of all lozts." *The Whole Body of Cookery*, dissected by William Rabisha, also has a chapter on "All manners of tarts" in it.

Colonial America was a typical place to make pies. As the nation expanded, more sweeteners like maple syrup, cane sugar, molasses, and honey became available (the Dutch and English imported honeybees to the U.S.). Early colonists made pumpkin, apple, pear, quince, and blueberry pies. Amelia Simmon's *American Cookery* (1796), the country's first cookbook, has a recipe for "Pumpkin Pudding" baked in a crust. This is one of the first recipes for the popular pumpkin pie in America.

New England earned its reputation as the "pie belt" for a good cause. In New England, pies were a staple food, and it was not unusual to have pie for breakfast. New ingredients and regional specialties arose as the nation moved west.

The Northern states gained popularity for their pumpkin pies, the Midwest for their cream and cheese pies, the Upper Plains for their tart berry pies modeled after Swedish tart berry pies, and the Southwest for their nut pies made from local pecan and walnut trees. Also, the Pennsylvania Dutch were renowned for their shoofly pie, Florida for their key lime pie, Kentucky for their chess pie, and the states south of the Mason-Dixon line for their sweet potato pies.

The pie plant, sometimes known as rhubarb, was in use by the middle of the 19th century. Three pie plant recipes may be found in *The Good Cheer Cookbook* (Chippewa Falls, Wisconsin, 1899). There are numerous pie recipes in *The 76: A Cook Book*, published in 1876 and edited by the ladies of Plymouth Church in Des Moines, Iowa. This book has recipes for coconut, cream, custard, lemon, and even vinegar pies.

The health movement caused a decline in pie consumption in the United States during the late 19th and early 20th centuries. In fact, pie received criticism. The essays "Why I have no cakes and pies on my table" (1905) and "Why I oppose pies" by Sarah Tyson Rorer were published in *Ladies Home Journal* (1900). In these writings, Mrs. Rorer claimed that "pies and cakes are indigestible" and that "the inside of a pie is deleterious."

Instant pudding mixes, canned fruit, and frozen and ready pie crusts had made making pies simpler by the middle of the 20th century. The popularity of chilled pie dishes like Black Bottom Pie increased as home refrigerators became more widespread. Pie recipes from the quickly growing food industry contained ingredients like Coca-Cola, Oreos, potato chips, and Ritz crackers. Today, we are rediscovering our pie-making roots and going back to the basics. Many of us are searching for vintage family recipes so we may recreate Grandma's pie.

Tips for Making the Perfect Pie

Unlike our grandmothers, we now have the advantage of the technology at our disposal. You have the choice to make pies the old-fashioned way or to use modern equipment. Following these basic tips will help you create tasty pies with great crusts every time!

Use fresh ingredients in the right proportions

Start with fresh, good-quality ingredients to ensure your pie will taste great. The usual proportion is 1:1 for flour to butter and about 1:2 for water to flour by weight. Another well-known conventional proportion of ingredients is 3-2-1: 3 parts flour, 2 parts fat, and 1 part water by weight. Too little butter will cause the dough to break easily and be difficult to handle. In warm climates, butter may be difficult to handle, so shortening may be used, although the resulting crust will not be as tasty. A heaping teaspoon of baking powder to 4 cups of flour can be a big help for the beginning pie maker to achieve a flaky crust.

Keep it cool

The secret to achieving a delicate, flaky crust is to keep things cool. Your flour, water, butter, and working surface should be cool. The main reason is to keep the pieces of butter in the dough from melting. The pieces of butter in the dough are what will melt upon baking, leaving layers of flakey crust.

Keep it light and quick

When handling the dough, be light and quick. Be gentle; rough handling will cause the butter and form a solid mass that will give you a tough crust.

Use your hands

Most recipes instruct that one use a pastry blender or two knives to combine the butter with the dry ingredients. The truly old-fashioned way is to rub the butter into the flour with the thumb and forefinger. Butter pieces in the flour the size of half a walnut will give a flaky crust ideal for fruit pies while making small, pea-sized lumps will make a shorter crust suitable for custard pies. If you have warm hands, run them under cold water and wipe them dry before handling the mixture.

Keep water to a minimum

You only need about 2 to 4 tablespoons of ice water for each cup of flour. A maximum would be about 50% of the amount of flour in your recipe by weight. Too much water will result in a hard and brittle crust. Too little will give a too-crumbly crust that will cause problems in slicing and serving when done.

Roll out the crust

The trick is still to move swiftly. Dusting the tabletop and rolling pin with flour keeps the dough from sticking. As too much flour can make the crust too tough, our grandmas used to line the work table with a kitchen towel and put the rolling pin in a stocking. You can use plastic to line these surfaces. Strokes in rolling should start from the center and go outward towards the edges. Use quick, light strokes. Heavy strokes cause sticking and breaking. The bottom crust should be about ⅛-inch thick, and the top crust slightly thinner. Roll the dough to about 14 inches in diameter and sling it over your pan. Gently press to make it conform to the shape of the pan. Do not stretch the dough as this will lead to shrinkage while baking. Trim off any excess. Roll the remaining dough to make a whole top crust or strips for the top.

Give it a rest

Cover the prepared crust with a kitchen towel and let it rest in a cool, dry area of your kitchen. Or cover it with plastic or foil and let it cool in the refrigerator for 30 minutes to an hour (some recommend 2 hours, with about 5 to 20 minutes of "thawing", or time to allow the dough to soften for easier handling). This relaxes the dough and ensures the butter does not form a tough mass with the dough. Our grandmothers used to wrap the dough with wax paper and put rice, beans, or another pie pan on top of the crust to help it keep its form while resting and chilling.

Glaze with egg white

Brush your lower crust with egg white to prevent the filling from making it soggy when it is baked. Brush more over the top crust to give it a nice, golden-brown sheen.

Let the steam off

Pies with juicy fillings need a way to let off steam without deforming the crust. Make several slits in the top crust to allow steam to escape while baking. Some bakers insert dried macaroni into the slits to act like little chimneys while the pie is baking. The top or bottom crust may be rolled about ½-inch longer than the other. The ½-inch excess can be folded over the other, and the two pressed together to seal. Moistening the edges or using a paste of flour and water can aid in sealing the edges. This will prevent filling from escaping from the sides of the pie. A little cornstarch may be added to the filling to thicken the juices and prevent them from spilling out of the crust.

Blind bake the crust

This means baking the crust on its own before putting it in the filling. It can help prevent the crust from getting soggy when baked with the filling, so it will remain crisp and flakey. Bake at 450°F for about 15 minutes; then reduce the heat to 375°F and then bake for about 5 to

10 minutes. It should just be light golden brown in color, not fully baked. Let it cool before adding the filling. To keep the crust from losing its shape while baking, line it with foil and fill it with beans or pie weights. The weight will keep the crust from puffing out of shape due to steam formed in air pockets within it.

For easy cleanup

For pies with fillings that tend to boil over, like savory stew fillings or fruit fillings with juice, place a baking tray underneath the pie to catch any drips and make for easier clean-up.

The right temperature

A hot oven at 450-475°F is the usual temperature to bake a pie crust. The pie crust should take about 15 minutes to reach a nice, delicate brown. As with blind baking, you may need to reduce the temperature to 375°F after the initial 15 minutes of baking and cook the pie longer until it is done and an even light golden brown in color. Placing a small piece of dough in the oven to test the temperature may be done as well. If the temperature is too high, the crust will be too dark and the pie unevenly baked. A temperature that is too low will give a pale, doughy crust, and the filling may not be cooked thoroughly.

To prevent a too-dark crust

Loosely covering the pie with foil can help prevent an over-darkening of the crust. You may remove the foil during the final minutes of baking to get a nice golden color.

Now it's time to try out the recipes in this cookbook! Here's a collection of good old-fashioned pie recipes, some you're familiar with and some you may have never even heard of. Each recipe will bring you back to times when pie makers had to use resourcefulness to come up with delicious pie treats. Other pies are influenced by the other cultures that have enriched our own. These pies reflect how America is truly a rich melting pot of cultures, and they demonstrate the spirit and ingenuity of the pioneers who concocted delicious pie recipes even during the hardest times.

Now that we have look at the tips for making the perfect pies, let's start baking!

Please note that, at the end of the book, in the appendix, you will find all the pie crust recipes needed to make your pies from scratch.

CUSTARD PIES

Egg Custard Pie

This pie is a 1990s American custard pie winner made with eggs, milk, and nutmeg.

Serves 8 | Prep. time 15 minutes | Cooking time 30-35 minutes

Ingredients
1 (9-inch) frozen pie crust, thawed
3 large eggs, beaten
¾ cup granulated sugar
1 teaspoon pure vanilla extract
¼ teaspoon kosher salt
2 ½ cups scalded milk
3 drops yellow food coloring (optional)
1 large egg white, beaten
¼ teaspoon ground nutmeg

Directions

1. Preheat the oven to 400°F (204°C).
2. Add the eggs, sugar, vanilla, and salt to a large mixing bowl. Mix until well-combined.
3. Add the scalded milk. If desired, add 3 drops of food coloring.
4. Brush the beaten egg white on the bottom and sides of the pie crust to prevent sogginess.
5. Transfer the custard mixture into the pie crust. Top with the nutmeg.
6. Bake for 30-35 minutes, or until a toothpick or knife inserted in the center of the cake comes out clean.
7. Place on a wire rack to cool before serving.

Nutrition (per serving)
Calories 252, fat 10 g, carbs 33 g, sugar 22 g, Protein 6 g, sodium 276.9 mg

Old-Fashioned Buttermilk Pie

Buttermilk pie is a silky custard-like pie using buttermilk and eggs, that came from English settlers at the end of the 18th century. My grandmother used to make it to finish up a buttermilk carton when I was a child. This is her recipe.

Serves 6-8 | Prep time 20 minutes | Cook time 1 hour 45 minutes

Ingredients
1 (9-inch) plain pastry pie shell, unbaked
3 tablespoons unsalted butter
1¼ cups white sugar
3 eggs
1 tablespoon flour
½ cup buttermilk
1 teaspoon vanilla

Directions

1. Preheat the oven to 300°F (149°C).
2. In a mixing bowl, cream together the butter and sugar.
3. Stir in the eggs, flour, buttermilk, and vanilla. Blend well.
4. Spread the filling in the pie shell.
5. Bake for about 1 hour and 45 minutes, or until a knife inserted in the filling comes out clean.
6. Let the pie cool before serving.

Nutrition (per serving)
Calories 285, fat 11 g, carbs 43 g, sugar 33 g,
Protein 4 g, sodium 125 mg

Flapper Pie

Another wonderful recipe that has been lost in time. My grandmother on my father's side used to make it often for her family. It was on all the menus in dinners restaurant in the 1920s. This recipe was written on a piece of paper that I found in an old cookbook my grandma gave me when I got married. I have made it a few times and it always impresses me.

Serves 6-8 | Prep. time 20 minutes | Cooking time 10-15 minutes

Ingredients
Graham Cracker Crust
1 ¼ cups graham cracker, finely crushed
¼ cup melted butter
½ cup sugar
Dash cinnamon

For the filling
2 ½ cups milk
½ cup white sugar
¼ cup cornstarch
3 egg yolks
1 teaspoon vanilla
Pinch salt

Meringue topping
¼ teaspoon cream of tartar
½ cup sugar
4 large egg whites, at room temperature
½ teaspoon vanilla extract

Directions
To make the crust

1. Mix the ingredients thoroughly. Set aside 2 tablespoons for garnish.
2. Press the mixture into a pie pan to form a shell and refrigerate to set.

To make the filling

3. In a saucepan, combine the filling ingredients and cook over medium heat, stirring constantly.
4. Continue cooking until the custard has thickened.
5. Allow the mixture to cool while preparing the meringue topping.

To make the meringue

6. In a large glass or metal bowl, whip the egg whites until they are foamy. Add the sugar gradually and continue to whip until stiff peaks form. Spread the meringue over the pie.

To assemble and bake

7. Preheat the oven to 350°F (177°C).
8. Spread the filling in the crust while it is still slightly warm and spoon the meringue on top.
9. Swirl the meringue with a fork and swirl to form peaks.
10. Bake until the meringue is golden brown (about 10-15 minutes). Sprinkle with the reserved crust mixture to garnish.

Nutrition (per serving)
Calories 291, fat 11 g, carbs 43 g, sugar 32 g,
Protein 7 g, sodium 139 mg

Chess Pie

The chess pie first appears in American cookbooks during the mid-18th century and originated in England well before. It's a luscious custard filling of buttermilk, sugar, and eggs. This is my aunt Eunice's recipe. It was passed down to her by her grandmother.

Serves 8 | Prep time 5 minutes | Cook time 50-55 minutes

Ingredients
1 (9-inch) plain pastry pie crust, prebaked
Powdered sugar, for garnish

<u>For the filling</u>
2 cups sugar
2 tablespoons cornmeal
1 tablespoon flour
¼ teaspoon salt
½ cup butter or margarine, melted
¼ cup milk
1 tablespoon white vinegar
½ teaspoon vanilla extract
4 eggs, well beaten

Directions

1. Preheat the oven to 350°F (177°C).
2. In a bowl, combine the ingredients for the filling EXCEPT for the eggs, whisking until well blended.
3. Stir in the eggs and stir to combine well.
4. Pour the mixture into the pie shell and place it in the oven.
5. After 10-15 minutes of baking, wrap the edges with aluminum foil and continue baking for 40-45 minutes.
6. Allow the pie to cool completely, then sift powdered sugar over the top if desired, and serve.

Nutrition (per serving)
Calories 476, fat 20 g, carbs 70 g, sugar 52 g,
Protein 4 g, sodium 226 mg

Tyler Pie

This pie was served at the White House during President John Tyler's tenure at the end of the 19th century. It was an old family recipe passed down from one generation to the next and originated in England. It's a rich custard pie that melts in your mouth. A favorite in our family too!

Serves 8 | Prep. time 10 minutes | Cooking time 35-40 minutes

Ingredients
1 (9-inch) plain pastry pie shell
1 cup sugar
½ teaspoon of flour
Pinch salt
2 eggs
1 teaspoon vanilla extract
½ teaspoon lemon extract
Pinch nutmeg
½ cup butter, slightly melted
1 cups milk

Directions

1. Preheat the oven to 350°F (177°C).
2. Combine the sugar, flour, and salt, and mix well.
3. In a separate bowl, beat the eggs and add the vanilla, lemon extract (optional), nutmeg, and butter. Stir in the sugar mixture.
4. Finally, mix in the milk. Pour the filling into an unbaked pie shell.
5. Bake until set and nicely browned (about 35-40 minutes).

Nutrition (per serving)
Calories 320, fat 18 g, carbs 37 g, sugar 28 g,

Protein 4 g, sodium 132 mg

Vinegar Pie

Cooks from the 19th century started using vinegar to flavor pies, especially in the North and Midwest of the Unites States. Vinegar was used to add a tart flavor to desserts when citrus, especially lemons were not available. I found this recipe in my grandmother's recipe box, and it seriously tastes like lemon pie!

Serves 8 | Prep. time 5 minutes | Cooking time 35 minutes

Ingredients
1 (9-inch) pie shell, pre-baked and cooled
3 tablespoons flour
1 cup sugar
⅓ cup white vinegar
1 ⅔ cups hot water
1 egg, well beaten
1 teaspoon lemon extract
2 tablespoons butter

Meringue topping
¼ teaspoon cream of tartar
½ cup sugar
4 large egg whites, at room temperature
½ teaspoon vanilla extract

Directions

1. Preheat the oven to 325°F (163°C).
2. Combine the sugar with the flour in a double boiler.
3. Whisk in the vinegar, water, egg, and lemon flavor.
4. Cook, stirring, in the double boiler until the mixture is thick.
5. Remove from the heat and stir in the butter.
6. Pour the filling into the pie shell.

7. To make the meringue, in a large glass or metal bowl, whip the egg whites until they are foamy. Add the sugar gradually and continue to whip until stiff peaks form.
8. Pile the meringue topping on the filling and spread to the edges of the pie. Use a fork to create swirls and peaks.
9. Bake until the meringue is golden brown (about 15 minutes). Serve hot.

Nutrition (per serving)
Calories 290, fat 8 g, carbs 51 g, sugar 39 g,
Protein 4 g, sodium 124 mg

Cream Pie

This simple, traditional cream pie is made with cream, butter, nutmeg, and sugar.

Serves 4 | Prep. time 15 minutes | Cooking time 45 minutes

Ingredients
1 (9-inch) pie shell, unbaked
1 cup granulated sugar
3 tablespoons all-purpose flour
½ teaspoon ground nutmeg
⅛ teaspoon kosher salt
1½ cups heavy cream
1 tablespoon unsalted butter
½ teaspoon pure vanilla extract

Directions

1. Preheat the oven to 400°F (204°C).
2. In a medium saucepan, add the sugar, flour, nutmeg, and salt over medium-low heat. Stir to combine.
3. Add the vanilla extract, butter, and milk. Combine, and cook for 3-5 minutes.
4. Transfer the mixture to the unbaked pie shell.
5. Bake for 10 minutes.
6. Lower the heat to 350°F (177°C). Bake for another 30 minutes or until the center rises.
7. Cool slightly before serving.

Nutrition (per serving)
Calories 295, fat 8 g, carbs 57 g, sugar 52 g,
Protein 1 g, sodium 124 mg

Boston Cream Pie

This classic Boston cream pie is beloved for its soft, creamy texture.

Serves 8 | Prep. time 15 minutes | Cooking time 15 minutes

Ingredients
1 (3-ounce) packet banana cream pudding and pie filling mix
1½ cups whole milk
½ cup cocoa, unsweetened
1 tablespoon oleo, softened
1 8-inch yellow layer cake, baked
½ cup whipped cream

Directions

1. Cook the pudding and milk per package directions.
2. Remove from heat and measure out 1 cup of the pudding.
3. In a medium mixing bowl, to make chocolate pudding, add the cocoa and oleo to the remaining pudding. Once oleo melts, combine and cool completely.
4. Cut the layer cake in half. Gently fold the whipped cream, sugar, and vanilla into the plain pudding.
5. Spread the plain pudding mixture evenly over the cake's bottom half.
6. Top with the other cake layer. Top with the chocolate pudding mixture.
7. Refrigerate until ready to serve.

Nutrition (per serving)
Calories 198, fat 9 g, carbs 25 g, sugar 19 g,
Protein 7 g, sodium 276 mg

CHOCOLATE PIES
Chocolate Custard Pie

This pie recipe is brimming with Southern tradition. It contains homemade chocolate custard and a meringue topping.

Serves 8 | Prep. time 15 minutes
Cooking time 10-12 minutes | Chill time 2 hours

Ingredients
1 (9-inch) pie shell, baked and cooled

For the custard
¾ cup granulated sugar
2 tablespoons self-rising flour
1 tablespoon cocoa powder
2 cups whole milk
2 large egg yolks
1 teaspoon pure vanilla extract

For the meringue
2 large egg whites
1 pinch granulated sugar
1 dash pure vanilla extract

Directions

1. Mix the sugar, flour, and cocoa powder thoroughly in a medium mixing bowl.
2. Combine the milk, egg yolks, and vanilla extract in a large mixing bowl until smooth.
3. Add the flour mixture and mix until well-combined.
4. Transfer the custard into a cast-iron skillet heated over medium heat.

5. Cook for 5-7 minutes while stirring constantly, until just barely boiling.
6. Remove from heat after cooking for another 3 to 5 minutes or until fairly thick.
7. Stir out any lumps in the hot custard before transferring it into the prepared pie shell.
8. Set an oven rack about 6 inches from the heat source and preheat the oven broiler.
9. Make the meringue by combining the egg whites, sugar, and vanilla extract in a small mixing bowl.
10. Beat using an electric mixer until soft peaks form.
11. Cover the custard with the meringue.
12. Bake the pie under a preheated broiler for 1-2 minutes, or until the meringue peaks start to turn light brown. Be careful not over-broil it.
13. To get the custard to congeal, refrigerate the custard pie for at least 2 hours, then serve.

Nutrition (per serving)
Calories 250, fat 10 g, carbs 34 g, sugar 19 g, Protein 5 g, sodium 182.2 mg

Chocolate Fudge Pie

This chocolate fudge pie is extra-decadent with its homemade rich filling.

Serves 8 | Prep. time 5 minutes | Cooking time 50 minutes

Ingredients
1 (9-inch) pie crust, refrigerated
½ cup unsalted butter
3 (1-ounce) squares chocolate, unsweetened
1½ cups granulated sugar
4 large eggs
3 tablespoons light corn syrup
1 teaspoon pure vanilla extract

Directions

1. Preheat the oven to 350°F (177°C).
2. In a saucepan over low heat, combine the butter and chocolate until melted.
3. Turn off the heat. Add the sugar, eggs, corn syrup, and vanilla extract. Stir until well-combined, then transfer the mixture into the pie crust.
4. Bake for about 40-45 minutes, or until somewhat jiggly and mainly set.
5. Before serving, let the pie reach room temperature so the filling can thicken further.

Nutrition (per serving)
Calories 475, fat 20 g, carbs 70 g, sugar 51 g
Protein 6 g, sodium 381 mg

Chocolate Chip Pie

This pie becomes popular in the 1980s. Its chocolate morsels made it an instant hit.

Serves 12 | Prep. time 5-10 minutes | Cooking time 30 minutes

Ingredients
1 (9-inch) deep-dish pie shell, unbaked
2 large eggs
½ cup all-purpose flour
½ cup granulated sugar
½ cup packed light brown sugar
¾ cup unsalted butter, melted and cooled to room temperature
6 ounces semi-sweet chocolate morsels
1 cup chopped walnuts
Sweetened whipped cream or ice cream, for serving

Directions

1. Preheat the oven to 325°F (163°C).
2. In a large mixing bowl, whisk the eggs until foamy.
3. Add the flour, granulated sugar, and brown sugar. Mix until well-combined.
4. Add the melted butter and combine well.
5. In a small mixing bowl, combine the walnuts and chocolate morsels. Add this mixture to the flour mixture and mix until well-combined.
6. Transfer the filling into the pie crust.
7. Bake for about 30 minutes or until the crust is golden-brown.
8. Serve warm with ice cream or whipped cream on top.

Nutrition (per serving)
Calories 390, fat 26 g, carbs 39 g, sugar 28 g,

Protein 5 g, sodium 137 mg

Chocolate Rum Pie

This layered chocolate pie first entered the scene in the 1970s.

Serves 9 | Prep. time 20 minutes
Cooking time 35 minutes | Chill time 2 hours

Ingredients
1 (9-inch) pie shell, baked and cooled
2 cups semi-sweet chocolate morsels
1 cup whole milk
¼ cup + ½ cup granulated sugar, divided
1 tablespoon gelatin, unflavored
½ teaspoon kosher salt
2 large eggs, separated
¼ cup rum
1 cup heavy cream
2 tablespoons powdered sugar

Directions

1. Using a double boiler, completely dissolve the gelatin. Add the chocolate chips, milk, ¼ cup sugar, and salt. Stir to combine.
2. Add the egg yolk quickly and cook, stirring constantly for another 2 minutes.
3. Remove the pot from the heat and stir in the rum.
4. Refrigerate the mixture for 1½ hours, or until thickened.
5. In a small mixing bowl, beat the egg whites until foamy.
6. Gradually add ½ cup sugar, beating thoroughly after each edition. Beat until stiff peaks form.
7. Fold the whipped cream into the cooled chocolate mixture, then set aside.
8. In a small mixing bowl, combine the heavy cream and powdered sugar. Beat until stiff peaks form.

9. Spread half the chocolate mixture into the pie crust.
10. Spread 1¼ cups whipped cream over the chocolate filling. Top with the remaining chocolate mixture.
11. Top with more leftover whipped cream. You can also use a pastry bag to pipe the whipped cream.
12. Refrigerate until completely set, then serve.

Nutrition (per serving)
Calories 326, fat 20 g, carbs 32 g, sugar 18 g,
Protein 5 g, sodium 250 mg

Chocolate Black Bottom Pie

This 1950s pie has an unusually fluffy texture.

Serves 12 | Prep. time 20 minutes
Cooking time 10 minutes | Chill time 4-5 hours

Ingredients
1 (9-inch) pie shell, baked and cooled
1 envelope gelatin, unflavored
¾ cup granulated sugar
⅛ teaspoon kosher salt
1 large egg yolk, slightly beaten
¾ cup whole milk
4 squares unsweetened chocolate, divided
1 cup ice-cold evaporated milk, whipped
1 teaspoon pure vanilla extract
1 cup whipped cream, sweetened

Directions

1. Combine the gelatin, sugar, and salt on top of a double boiler.
2. To the gelatin mixture, add the egg yolk and milk. Stir to combine.
3. Add 3 of the chocolate squares.
4. Cook the chocolate over boiling water, stirring frequently, until melted.
5. Remove from the heat. Transfer the mixture to a medium mixing bowl and beat with a hand mixer.
6. Refrigerate until thickened, about 30 minutes.
7. Gently fold in the vanilla extract and whipped evaporated milk.
8. Transfer the mixture into the pie crust.

9. Refrigerate the pie for at least 4-5 hours or until thick and set.
10. Top the pie with whipped cream. Using a peeler, shave the remaining 1 square of chocolate into long curls. Then, arrange the widest curls upright, sprinkle them over the pie, and serve.

Nutrition (per serving)
Calories 158, fat 8 g, carbs 19 g, sugar 15 g,
Protein 4 g, sodium 112 mg

Frozen Mud Pie

This is a pie chocolate lovers will surely love. It may look complicated but fear not. It is so easy to make than it looks that you'll soon enjoy this pie in no time.

Serves 8 | Prep time 15 minutes | Chill time 30 minutes

Ingredients
1½ cups Oreo cookie crumbs
1½ teaspoons sugar
¼ cup butter, melted
4-5 cups chocolate ice cream, softened
½ cup chocolate syrup, plus more for serving
Crushed nuts, for serving
Whipped cream, for serving

Directions

1. For the crust, in a small bowl, blend together the cookie crumbs and sugar.
2. Add the butter and mix well.
3. Place the mixture into an ungreased 8-inch pie dish evenly.
4. With the back of a spoon, press onto the bottom and up the sides of the pie dish.
5. Refrigerate for about 30 minutes.
6. Remove the pie dish from the oven and place half of the ice cream into the crust.
7. Drizzle the ice cream with half of the chocolate syrup evenly.
8. With a knife, swirl the chocolate syrup.
9. Gently place the remaining ice cream on top and drizzle with the remaining chocolate syrup.
10. Freeze the pie dish until firm.

11. Remove the pie dish from the freezer and set it aside for about 10–15 minutes before serving. Top with whipped cream, chocolate syrup, and crushed nuts if desired.

Nutrition (per serving)
Calories 293, fat 21 g, carbs 23 g, sugar 17 g,
Protein 2 g, sodium 143 mg

Banoffee Pie

The Hungry Monk Restaurant in East Sussex takes the credit for inventing this great-tasting Banoffee pie in the 1970s. As one could predict, it became hugely popular, and since then it has become a permanent fixture on the restaurant's menu.

Serves 8 | Prep. time 20 minutes
Cooking time 5 minutes | Chilling time 7 hours

Ingredients

3 cups chocolate wafers or chocolate digestive cookies
½ cup unsalted butter, melted
1 cup caramel sauce or dulce de leche
2 bananas, peeled and sliced
1½ cups chilled heavy whipping cream
¼ cup confectioners' sugar or powdered sugar
1 teaspoon vanilla extract
2 ounces chocolate curls, chunks, or chocolate chips

Directions

1. Grease an 8-inch pie pan with some butter or cooking oil.
2. In a food processor, process the cookies into crumbs.
3. Place the crumbs in a Ziploc bag and crush them with a rolling pin.
4. Melt the butter in a medium saucepan or skillet over medium heat.
5. Add the crumbs and mix well.
6. Add the mixture to the pie pan and press to make a ¼-inch-thick crust. Refrigerate for 4 hours.
7. Melt the chocolate in a double broiler. Pour it over the crust to make a thin layer.
8. Refrigerate for 1 hour more.
9. Use a knife to create curls over the chocolate layer.

10. Pour on the caramel sauce or dulce de leche and spread evenly.
11. Arrange the sliced bananas over it.
12. Combine the heavy cream, vanilla, and icing sugar until well blended.
13. Pour the mixture over the bananas. Top with chocolate curls/chunks/chips.
14. Refrigerate for a final 2 hours.
15. Slice and serve.

Nutrition (per serving)
Calories 634, fat 37 g, carbs 73 g, sugar 51 g,
Protein 5 g, sodium 271 mg

Possum Pie

This vintage possum pie is so creamy and indulgent. It contains cream cheese and layered chocolate filling inside a pecan shortbread crust.

Serves 10 | Prep. time 20 minutes
Cooking time 25 minutes | Chill time 4 hours 30 minutes

Ingredients
<u>For the crust</u>
1 cup all-purpose flour
½ cup unsalted butter
¼ cup light brown sugar
¾ cup chopped pecans

<u>For the cream cheese layer</u>
6 ounces cream cheese, softened
½ cup powdered sugar
2 tablespoons heavy cream

<u>For the pudding layer</u>
1 cup granulated sugar
⅓ cup cocoa powder
3 tablespoons corn starch
2 tablespoons all-purpose flour
Pinch of kosher salt
3 large egg yolks
2 cups whole milk
2 tablespoons unsalted butter
1 teaspoon pure vanilla extract

<u>For the topping</u>
½ cup heavy whipping cream
2 tablespoons powdered sugar

½ teaspoon pure vanilla extract
1-2 tablespoons chopped pecans
Grated chocolate of choice

Directions

1. To make the crust, preheat the oven to 350°F (177°C).
2. In a medium saucepan, melt the butter over medium heat, stirring regularly. Add the flour, brown sugar, and pecans into the melted butter and whisk until well combined.
3. Fill a well-greased (9-inch) pie plate with the mixture.
4. Bake for 15-20 minutes, or until the crust is golden-brown. Let the crust cool completely on a wire rack.
5. To make the filling: in a medium mixing bowl, beat together the cream cheese, powdered sugar, and heavy cream with a hand mixer.
6. Spread the cream cheese mixture across the bottom of the cooled crust.
7. To make the chocolate layer: in a medium saucepan over medium heat, add the sugar, cocoa powder, cornstarch, flour, and salt. Whisk until well-combined.
8. In a small bowl, whisk together the egg yolks and milk. Add them to the sugar and cocoa powder mixture.
9. Cook the pudding, whisking constantly, over medium heat for 7 to 10 minutes, or until thickened and bubbling.
10. Remove the saucepan from the heat and stir in the vanilla extract. Transfer the chocolate pudding to a shallow bowl and cover it with plastic wrap. This step will prevent a "skin" from forming over the pudding.
11. Refrigerate the filling for 30 minutes.
12. Remove the plastic wrap from the filling and whisk the pudding thoroughly. Transfer the filling over the cream cheese layer.

13. Cover the pie with plastic wrap and refrigerate for 4 hours or until set.
14. To make the topping: add the heavy cream, powdered sugar, and vanilla to a medium mixing bowl. Using a hand mixer, beat until stiff peaks form. The peaks should maintain their shape after you remove the beaters.
15. Spread the whipped cream over the chocolate pudding layer. Top with the chopped pecans and shaved chocolate before slicing and serving.

Nutrition (per serving)
Calories 513, fat 32 g, carbs 52 g, sugar 36 g,
Protein 7 g, sodium 188 mg

Whoopie Pies

Whoopie pies are a popular Pennsylvania Amish tradition and also a New England phenomenon. They're a real comfort food often enjoyed with a glass of milk. This vintage pie dates back to 1925, when Labadie's Bakery in Lewiston, Maine, started selling it soon after it opened. A fluffy white filling makes this pie creamier than ever. The dark brown crust is made from soft cookies. As per Amish legend, this pie got its name because children used to cheer "whoopee!" whenever they found it in their lunch bags.

Serves 8 | Prep. time 30 minutes | Cooking time 60 minutes

Ingredients

1¼ teaspoons baking soda
1 teaspoon salt
2 cups all-purpose flour
½ cup cocoa powder
1 cup buttermilk
½ cup (1 stick) unsalted butter, softened
1 teaspoon vanilla
1 large egg
1 cup packed brown sugar

Filling
½ cup (1 stick) unsalted butter, softened
2 cups marshmallow cream
1¼ cups confectioners' sugar
1 teaspoon vanilla

Directions

1. Preheat the oven to 350°F (177°C). Grease two baking sheets with cooking spray or melted butter.

2. Whisk the flour, cocoa, baking soda, and salt in a medium-large bowl.
3. Combine the buttermilk and vanilla in another bowl.
4. Beat the butter and brown sugar in a third bowl until the sugar dissolves.
5. Add the eggs and combine well.
6. Alternately add the buttermilk and flour mixture in batches, mixing continuously until you get a smooth mixture.
7. Place ¼-cup mounds of the mixture on the baking sheets, keeping a 2-inch interval between them.
8. Bake both sheets simultaneously, one above the other, for about 12 minutes or until the tops of the pies are puffed, switching the top and bottom sheets halfway through.
9. Let cool completely.
10. Prepare the filling by whisking the filling ingredients in a mixing bowl for 2–3 minutes.
11. Arrange half of the prepared cakes, spread the filling over them, and top with the remaining cakes.

Nutrition (per serving)
Calories 504, fat 14 g, carbs 92 g, sugar 56 g,
Protein 6 g, sodium 362 mg

Cocoa Cream Pie

This pie will undoubtedly become a crowd favorite. It's also so simple to make with just cocoa powder, whipped cream, and a delicious crust. It`s from the 1970s era where crem pie were so popular. I found this one in my mom recipe box, handwritten. It has become one of our favorite.

Serves 8 | Prep. time 10 minutes | Cooking time 20 minutes

Ingredients
1 (9-inch) shortcrust pie shell, prebaked
½ cup cocoa
1¼ cups sugar
⅓ cup cornstarch
¼ teaspoon salt
3 cups milk
3 tablespoons butter
1½ teaspoons vanilla
Sweetened whipped cream

Directions

1. In a saucepan over medium heat, mix cocoa, sugar, salt, and cornstarch. Slowly add milk until well combined.
2. Let it boil for 1 minute then remove from heat.
3. Add butter and vanilla. Mix until well combined.
4. Spread mixture over the pie crust.
5. Cover with plastic wrap and press onto the filling.
6. Refrigerate for 3 to 4 hours.
7. Before serving, remove the plastic wrap and top with whipped cream then serve.

Nutrition (per serving)
Calories 345, fat 14 g, carbs 55 g, sugar 37 g, Protein 6 g, sodium 195 mg

Marshmallow and Chocolate Pie

Marshmallows and chocolate are such an irresistible combination. Your guests will surely find it hard to say no to a second or even a third slice of this delicious pie. It became popular in the 1980s when lots of desserts were inspired by Smore`s!

Serves 8 | Prep. time 10 minutes
Chill time 3 hours 10 minutes

Ingredients
1 (9-inch) graham cracker crust
20 marshmallows
½ cup milk
7 ½ ounces milk chocolate with almonds
½ pint whipped cream

Directions

1. In a pot over medium heat, melt marshmallows, chocolate, and milk. Stir until well combined.
2. Freeze for 10 minutes. Stir in whipped cream.
3. Pour onto the crust then chill the pie for 3 hours.

Nutrition (per serving)
Calories 338, fat 17 g, carbs 44 g, sugar 29 g,
Protein 4 g, sodium 135 mg

SUGAR AND OTHER SWEET PIES

Sugar Cream Pie

This pie recipe originally came from Huntington, Indiana. It is as sweet and smooth as butter.

Serves 8 | Prep. time 20 minutes | Cooking time 1 hour

Ingredients
1 (9-inch) plain pastry pie shell
2 cups heavy cream
½ cup all-purpose flour
½ cup dark brown sugar
½ cup + 3 tablespoons granulated sugar, divided
½ cup whole milk
1 teaspoon pure vanilla extract
1 (9-inch) pie crust, unbaked
1 tablespoon unsalted butter
1 teaspoon ground cinnamon

Directions

1. Preheat the oven to 350°F (177°C).
2. In a medium mixing bowl, combine the heavy cream, flour, brown sugar, ½ cup granulated sugar, milk, and vanilla extract.
3. Spread the prepared pie crust over a (9-inch) pie plate, then top with the butter.
4. Pour the filling into the crust. Add the remaining 3 tablespoons of sugar along with the cinnamon.
5. Bake for 1 hour, or until the center is set. Place on a wire rack to cool before serving.

Nutrition (per serving)

Calories 418, fat 24 g, carbs 47 g, sugar 28 g,
Protein 4 g, sodium 275 mg

Indiana Sugar Cream Pie

One of the things I love about vintage recipes is that they use ingredients we tend to have on hand. This recipe, for instance, is a good choice when you feel like having custard, but don't have (or want to use) any eggs. We suggest good quality cream, vanilla, and nutmeg—but in the spirit of the recipe, use what you have.

Serves 8 | Prep. time 10 minutes | Cooking time 40 minutes

Ingredients

For the crust
1⅔ cups all-purpose flour
2 tablespoons sugar
¼ teaspoon salt
¼ teaspoon baking powder
½ cup butter
2 large eggs, lightly beaten

For the filling
1½ cups heavy cream
½ cup milk
1 teaspoon vanilla extract
½ cup all-purpose flour
1 cup sugar
½ teaspoon salt
1 tablespoon butter, finely chopped
Freshly grated nutmeg

Directions

1. In a mixing bowl, combine the flour, sugar, salt, and baking powder. Mix well.
2. Cut in the butter until a coarse meal is formed. Add the eggs and mix until the pastry comes together. Wrap and

refrigerate for one hour.
3. Roll out the dough for a (9-inch) pie plate. Trim and flute the edges. Place the pie shell in the freezer.
4. Preheat the oven to 425°F (218°C).
5. Make the filling. In a bowl, mix the cream, milk, and vanilla.
6. In a separate bowl, combine the flour, sugar, and salt.
7. Slowly whisk the milk mixture into the flour mixture until combined.
8. Remove the pie crust from the freezer. Scatter the butter pieces over the bottom of the crust, and season with some nutmeg.
9. Whisk the batter again and carefully pour it into the crust. Place the pie on the middle rack in the preheated oven.
10. Bake for 10 minutes, and then open the oven door. Using a fork, carefully stir the filling, being careful not to damage the bottom of the pie.
11. Turn the heat down to 325°F (163°C) and bake until it is set, about 30 minutes.
12. Remove the pie to a cooling rack and sprinkle with some more nutmeg. Cool, and serve.

Nutrition (per serving)
Calories 522, fat 30 g, carbs 56 g, sugar 30 g,
Protein 7 g, sodium 272 mg

Maple Syrup Pie

This delectable maple syrup pie is made with pure maple syrup and butter.

Serves 8 | Prep. time 30 minutes | Cooking time 1 hour

Ingredients
2 plain pastry pie crust shells
3 tablespoons corn starch
⅔ cup water
1½ cups maple syrup
2 tablespoons unsalted butter

Directions

1. Preheat the oven to 400°F (204°C).
2. Combine the corn starch, water, and syrup in a large saucepan over medium heat. Bring to a boil, then simmer and stir for 4 minutes or until smooth and thickened. Then, add the butter and stir until melted
3. On a lightly dusted surface, roll out the bottom crust pie dough to a circle that is ⅛-inch thick. Transfer the round to a (9-inch) pie pan. Trim the crust at the plate's rim and flute the edges. Let it rest for at least 30 minutes to cool fully.
4. In the meantime, roll out the remaining dough to a thickness of ¼-inch, then use 1½ to 2½-inch cookie cutters to form maple leaf shapes. Transfer the shapes to a baking sheet.
5. Put the prepared pie filling in the pan. Bake on the bottom oven rack for 10 minutes.
6. Reduce the temperature to 350°F (177°C) and bake for another 35 to 40 minutes, or until the filling is bubbling and the crust is golden-brown.

7. Transfer the pie to a wire rack to cool completely. In the meantime, bake the maple leaf shapes for 10 minutes.
8. Place the baked maple leaf shapes on top of the pie before serving.

Nutrition (per serving)
Calories 536, fat 26 g, carbs 73 g, sugar 37 g,
Protein 4 g, sodium 340 mg

Butterscotch Pie

Delicious and easy to make, this sweet butterscotch pie makes a crowd-pleasing dessert, especially during the holidays. Aunt Eunice would bring it to potluck often. A perfect way to make anyone fall in love with butterscotch.

Serves 8 | Prep. time 10 minutes | Cooking time 10 minutes
Chill time 2-4 hours

Ingredients
1 recipe shortcrust pie shell, prebaked
2 tablespoons butter, melted
1 cup brown sugar
4 tablespoons milk
Whipped cream or meringue, for topping

Other ingredients
1 egg yolk
1 tablespoon corn starch
1 cup milk
Whipped cream

Directions

1. In a large bowl, mix butter, brown sugar, and milk.
2. In a pot, mix egg yolk, cornstarch, and milk and bring to a boil over medium high heat. Let the mixture cool for a few minutes.
3. Pour the milk mixture and whisk until the brown sugar mixture is smooth and well incorporated. Pour into the prebaked pie crust. Refrigerate for 2-4 hours.
4. Top with whipped cream and serve.

Nutrition (per serving)
Calories 236, fat 10 g, carbs 35 g, sugar 24 g,
Protein 3 g, sodium 107 mg

Burnt Caramel Pie

If you'd like a change from the usual butterscotch pie, try this throwback family recipe of ours. It's delicious!

Makes 2 pies | Prep. time 30 minutes
Chilling time 1 hour | Cooking time 30 minutes

Ingredients
For the crust
2 ⅔ cups all-purpose flour
2 tablespoons sugar
½ teaspoon salt
½ cup cold, unsalted butter, cubed
6 tablespoons cold vegetable shortening
2 teaspoons vinegar
½ cup ice water

For the filling
4 eggs, separated
1 cup evaporated milk
½ cup light corn syrup
¼ cup butter, melted
½ teaspoon vanilla extract
3 cups white sugar, divided
½ cup all-purpose flour
3 cups water
½ teaspoon cream of tartar

Directions

1. Prepare the crusts. In a large bowl, combine the flour, sugar, and salt. Cut in the butter and vegetable shortening with a pastry cutter or two knives until the mixture has pea-sized crumbs.

2. Gradually mix in the water just until the dough comes together. Be careful not to overwork the dough. Divide it in half and shape both into disks. Wrap in plastic and refrigerate for at least an hour.
3. Preheat the oven to 375°F (191°C) and set out two (9-inch) pie plates.
4. Roll the dough into two 12-inch circles and arrange one on each pie plate. Trim and flute the edges. Place a piece of foil in each pastry shell and fill them with dry beans or pie weights.
5. Bake for 15 minutes and then remove the foil and weights. Continue to bake the crusts for 10 more minutes, or until golden. Set them aside to cool.
6. Combine the egg yolks, evaporated milk, syrup, melted butter, vanilla, half a cup of sugar, and flour.
7. Heat the oven to 325°F (163°C).
8. Heat a cast iron skillet and brown 2 cups of the sugar until golden. Remove the pan from the heat and stir in the water. Stir until the sugar dissolves, returning the skillet to the heat.
9. Whisk in the egg yolk mixture and cook until it thickens, and then five minutes more. Pour the filling into the prepared pie shells.
10. Beat the egg whites until foamy. Add the cream of tartar and gradually beat in the remaining half cup of sugar. Beat until stiff peaks form and spread the meringue over the pies.
11. Bake for 15 minutes, until the meringue is golden.

Nutrition (per serving)
Calories 424, fat 16 g, carbs 68 g, sugar 47 g,
Protein 5 g, sodium 115 mg

Jefferson Davis Pie

Created in the honor of President Jefferson during the civil war era, this pie is decadent and a close cousin to the chess pie consisting of a brown sugar custard with dates, raisins, and pecans. It's delicious and won't stay for long. I found this recipe in my aunt's recipe box and have done it regularly over the years.

Serves 8 | Prep. time 10 minutes | Cooking time 55 minutes

Ingredients
1 (9-inch) plain pastry pie shell
½ cup golden raisins
½ cup chopped dates
½ cup pecans
3 tablespoons flour
1 teaspoon cinnamon
¼ teaspoon allspice
Pinch ground nutmeg
½ teaspoon salt
1 cup light brown sugar
1 stick unsalted butter, softened
1 cup light brown sugar
5 large egg yolks
1½ cups heavy cream
Whipped cream, for garnish

Directions

1. Preheat the oven to 325°F (163°C).
2. Place the raisins, dates, and pecans in a food processor or blender and run it until the mixture is finely ground. Spread this over the bottom of the pie shell.
3. Mix the flour, cinnamon, allspice, nutmeg, and salt together. Set it aside.

4. Cream the butter and brown sugar in a mixer. Add the yolks one at a time, mixing until well blended.
5. Add the flour mixture and cream alternately, stirring to combine.
6. Pour the filling into the pie shell.
7. Bake until the filling has thickened but is not too firm (about 55 minutes).
8. Serve chilled, topped with whipped cream.

Nutrition (per serving)
Calories 586, fat 41 g, carbs 54 g, sugar 38 g,
Protein 6 g, sodium 259 mg

Oatmeal Pie

Oatmeal pies were commonly made when pecans were hard to come by, like during the Civil war, as bakers replace the nuts with oatmeal. My great aunt Mary used to make it often. I barely remember as I was very young, but this is her recipe. It has the same sweet taste as pecan pie and its texture.

Serves 8 | Prep. time 5 minutes | Cooking time 45 minutes

Ingredients
1 (9-inch) plain pastry pie shell
1 cup sugar
2 tablespoons flour
1 teaspoon ground cinnamon
¼ teaspoon salt
4 eggs, beaten until frothy
1 cup light corn syrup
¼ cup melted butter
1 teaspoon vanilla
1 cup quick-cooking oatmeal, uncooked

Directions

1. Preheat the oven to 350°F (177°C).
2. Mix together the sugar, flour, cinnamon, and salt in a small bowl.
3. Stir in the eggs, corn syrup, melted butter, vanilla, and oatmeal.
4. Pour the mixture into the pie shell.
5. Bake for 45 minutes, or until set.

Nutrition (per serving)
Calories 431, fat 14 g, carbs 76 g, sugar 58 g,
Protein 5 g, sodium 216 mg

Mock Apple Pie

An apple pie without pies? This is a fun pie everyone should try out at least once. Serve it warm and you surely won't ask for anything else but maybe another slice of this.

Serves 8 | Prep. time 10 minutes
Cooling time 30 minutes | Cooking time 40-45 minutes

Ingredients
Pastry for double crust pie
1½ cups sugar
1 teaspoon cream of tartar
1 ¼ cups water
2 tablespoons lemon juice
18 saltines or 36 Ritz® crackers, halved
1 teaspoon ground cinnamon
½ teaspoon ground nutmeg
1-2 tablespoons butter
1-2 tablespoons butter
Milk or beaten egg, for glaze (optional)

Directions

1. Preheat the oven to 425°F (218°C).
2. In a saucepan, mix together the sugar and cream of tartar.
3. Gradually stir in the water and bring to a boil over high heat.
4. Reduce the heat to low, and simmer until the mixture is reduced to 1½ cups (about 5 minutes).
5. Stir in the lemon juice.
6. Remove the pot from the heat and let it cool (about 30 minutes).
7. Arrange the saltines or Ritz® crackers in the pie shell.

8. Pour the sugar syrup over the crackers, and sprinkle with cinnamon and nutmeg.
9. Dot with butter.
10. Cover with the top crust. Trim and flute the edge and cut slits to serve as vents. Brush with milk or egg to glaze (optional).
11. Bake until golden brown (30-35 minutes).
12. Let the pie cool before serving.

Nutrition (per serving)
Calories 361, fat 14 g, carbs 57 g, sugar 38 g,
Protein 3 g, sodium 143 mg

SPECIAL OCCASION PIES

Mincemeat Pie

Traditionally made at Christmas, these are treats that are well worth the effort. Canned or bottled mincemeat has simplified many recipes, but today we'll show you how to make the filling from scratch.

Serves 8 | Prep. time 20 minutes | Cooking time 1 hour

Ingredients
2 (9-inch) pie shells
2 ½ cups mincemeat, homemade (recipe below)
Brandy, to taste (optional)

<u>Homemade Mincemeat</u>
2 pounds venison, elk, or beef chunks
½ pound suet, finely chopped
Water, to cover
½ cup apple cider vinegar
6 whole cloves
6 whole allspices
1 large bay leaf
3 quarts apple cider
2 cups beef broth
3 pounds apples, chopped
3 pounds raisins (dark and golden)
2 pounds currants
½ pound citron
1 tablespoon ground cloves
1 tablespoon ground cinnamon
1 tablespoon ground nutmeg
1 tablespoon ground allspice

1 firmly packed cup brown sugar
2 cups rum or Applejack brandy

Directions
To make the mincemeat

1. Boil meat and suet together until tender (about 2 hours). Drain and cool, and then chop or grind the meat.
2. Combine all the other ingredients EXCEPT the brandy and simmer them for 1½ hours.
3. Stir in the brandy.
4. Store the mixture in quart-sized sterile jars. Seal and store refrigerated or frozen. Best when stored for 2 weeks before using.

To assemble and bake

5. Preheat the oven to 425°F (218°C).
6. Spoon the mincemeat into a pastry-lined pie plate.
7. Add brandy to taste (optional).
8. Cover with the top pastry, and trim and flute or crimp. Cut slits as vents and wrap the edge with aluminum foil to prevent the crust from getting too dark.
9. Bake until the crust is lightly browned (about 50 minutes) and remove the aluminum foil.
10. Bake 15 minutes more.
11. Cool on a wire rack before cutting.
12. Serve warm.

Nutrition (per serving)
Calories 1857, fat 44 g, carbs 336 g, sugar 245 g, Protein 38 g, sodium 540 mg

Pumpkin Pie

A perfect addition to any Thanksgiving feast, this pumpkin pie is so simple to make and the perfect ending to any mail. Garnish it with some sweetened whipped cream, if you like.

Serves 8 | Prep. time 5 minutes | Cooking time 1 hour

Ingredients
1 (9-inch) plain pastry pie shell
2 eggs, lightly beaten
2 cups pumpkin puree
¾ cup sugar
½ teaspoon salt
1 teaspoon cinnamon
½ teaspoon ground ginger
¼ teaspoon ground cloves
1 (12 ounces) can evaporated milk

Directions

1. Preheat the oven to 425°F (218°C).
2. In a mixing bowl, combine all the ingredients together.
3. Pour the mixture into a pie shell.
4. Bake for 15 minutes and then reduce the oven temperature to 350°F (177°C).
5. Continue baking until a knife inserted in the center of the filling comes out clean (about 45 minutes).
6. Let the pie cool before serving.

Nutrition (per serving)
Calories 256, fat 9 g, carbs 40 g, sugar 22 g,
Protein 6 g, sodium 293 mg

No-Bake Pumpkin Pie

This no-bake pumpkin pie became popular in the 1970s. Its gelatin gives it a smooth, velvety texture.

Serves 8 | Prep. time 5 minutes
Cooking time 15 minutes | Chill time 3 hours 30 minutes

Ingredients
1 (9-inch) pie shell, baked and cooled
½ cup granulated sugar
1 envelope gelatin, unflavored
1 teaspoon pumpkin spice
½ teaspoon kosher salt
1 cup whole milk
1 large egg, slightly beaten
1 (15-ounce) canned pumpkin
1 cup Cool Whip

Directions

1. In a medium saucepan, combine the sugar, gelatin, salt, and pumpkin pie spice.
2. Add the milk and stir to combine.
3. Cook the mixture over medium heat while constantly stirring.
4. In a medium bowl, transfer the beaten egg. Gradually combine the saucepan mixture with the egg.
5. Add the pumpkin and stir until completely thick.
6. Refrigerate until thickened, at least 30 minutes. Gently fold the Cool Whip into the mixture.
7. Transfer the mixture to the pie shell. Refrigerate for at least 3 hours or until set.
8. If desired, decorate the pie with a border of chopped walnuts and raisins before serving.

Nutrition (per serving)
Calories 170, fat 5 g, carbs 27 g, sugar 18 g,
Protein 4 g, sodium 206 mg

Pumpkin Chiffon Pie

This pumpkin chiffon pie is a no-bake filling pie made with gelatin.

Serves 8 | Prep. time 5 minutes
Cooking time 10-15 minutes | Chill time 30 minutes

Ingredients
1 (9-inch) pie shell, baked and cooled
1 envelope gelatin, unflavored
¾ cup packed dark brown sugar
½ teaspoon kosher salt
½ teaspoon ground nutmeg
1 teaspoon ground cinnamon
½ cup whole milk
¼ cup water
3 large eggs, divided
1½ cups canned pumpkin
¼ cup granulated sugar
Whipped cream, for serving

Directions

1. Add the gelatin, brown sugar, salt, nutmeg, and cinnamon to a medium bowl. Mix until well-combined then set the bowl over a large saucepan (this will make a double boiler). Set the heat level to medium heat and bring it to a boil.
2. In the meantime, in a large mixing bowl, combine the pumpkin, milk, water, and egg yolks. Add this mixture to the saucepan.
3. Cook for about 10 minutes, stirring occasionally, over boiling water, or until the gelatin dissolves and the mixture is heated through.

4. Remove from heat and set aside to let it cool. When sufficiently cool, the mixture should form a mound when you spoon it into it.
5. In the meantime, beat the egg whites in a large mixing bowl until stiff peaks form. Carefully fold in the sugar and the gelatin mixture.
6. Transfer the filling to the prepared pie crust and refrigerate for at least 30 minutes or until set.
7. If desired, top with whipped cream before serving.

Nutrition (per serving)
Calories 209, fat 4 g, carbs 39 g, sugar 28 g,
Protein 5 g, sodium 205 mg

Easy Streusel Pumpkin Pie

Savor every bite of this creamy pumpkin pie. You'll surely ask for more. It was a popular recipe when my mom was growing up and she wrote the recipe down on her precious cards. And I am so happy to share it with my family during the holidays. It's the streusel topping that makes it extra special.

Serves 8 | Prep. time 10 minutes | Cooking time 20 minutes

Ingredients
2 (9-inch) deep dish pie shells, frozen
2 large eggs
1 (16 ounces) can pumpkin purée
1 (12 ounces) can evaporated milk
¾ cup + 2 tablespoons sugar, divided
3 teaspoons pumpkin pie spice, divided
¼ cup walnuts, chopped

Directions

1. Preheat the oven to 375°F (191°C).
2. In a bowl, mix milk, ¾ cup sugar, and 2 teaspoons pumpkin spice. Pour the mixture into a pie crust.
3. Bake for 30 minutes.
4. Crumble into small pieces the second crust while still frozen. Add remaining sugar, pumpkin spice, and walnuts. Mix until well combined
5. Sprinkle onto the filling.
6. Bake for 30-40 minutes more, until a knife inserted in the middle comes out clean.
7. Cool pie first before serving.

Nutrition (per serving)

Calories 354, fat 17 g, carbs 44 g, sugar 21 g, Protein 7 g, sodium 269 mg

Italian Easter Pie

Easter Pie comes in many varieties, some savory and some sweet. This is an old family recipe that has probably been changed subtly over time, and now includes chocolate chips as well as more traditional ingredients like citron.

Serves 6–8 | Prep. time 25 minutes | Cooking time 55 minutes

Ingredients
For the crust
1 ⅔ cups all-purpose flour
2 tablespoons sugar
¼ teaspoon salt
¼ teaspoon baking powder
½ cup butter
2 large eggs, lightly beaten
Icing sugar for dusting

For the filling
2 cups ricotta cheese
1 cup sugar
1 tablespoon cornstarch
½ teaspoon grated lemon zest
½ teaspoon grated orange zest
¼ teaspoon salt
4 large eggs
2 teaspoons vanilla extract
⅓ cup semisweet chocolate chips
⅓ cup diced citron, optional
Pinch ground cinnamon
Pinch ground nutmeg

Directions

1. In a mixing bowl, combine the flour, sugar, salt, and baking powder. Mix well.
2. Cut in the butter until a coarse meal is formed. Add the eggs and mix until the pastry comes together. Wrap and refrigerate for one hour.
3. Roll out the dough for a (9-inch) pie plate. Trim and flute the edges. Refrigerate until ready to use.
4. Preheat the oven to 350°F (177°C).
5. To make the filling, beat the ricotta with the sugar and cornstarch. Mix in the lemon and orange zest and the salt.
6. In a separate bowl, beat the eggs until they are thick and pale yellow, about 5 minutes. Gently fold them into the ricotta mixture together with the remaining ingredients.
7. Pour the filling into the crust and bake for 55 minutes, or until a knife inserted in the center comes out clean.
8. Let cool and refrigerate for 1 hour prior to serving. Dust pie with icing sugar before serving.

Nutrition (per serving)
Calories 501, fat 24 g, carbs 60 g, sugar 35 g,
Protein 12 g, sodium 209 mg

Fruit Cocktail Eggnog Pie

This 1950s eggnog pie is made with fruit cocktail, gelatin, eggnog, and cream during the holiday season.

Serves 10 | Prep. time 30 minutes
Cooking time 5 minutes | Chill time 2-4 hours

Ingredients

1 (9-inch) pie shell, baked and cooled
3 ½ cups fruit cocktail
1 envelope gelatin, unflavored
1½ cups eggnog, prepared
⅛ teaspoon kosher salt
1½ teaspoons pure vanilla extract
¼ teaspoon almond flavoring
1 cup whipping cream

Directions

1. Drain the fruit cocktail, reserving ½ cup of the syrup in a large mixing bowl.
2. Add the gelatin to the syrup and stir to combine.
3. Place the gelatin bowl over a pot of boiling water and stir until the gelatin dissolves.
4. Remove from heat and stir in the eggnog.
5. Add the salt, vanilla extract, and almond flavoring. Stir to combine well.
6. Refrigerate the mixture until thickened (a spoonful of it should form a mound).
7. In a small mixing bowl, whip the cream until stiff peaks form.
8. Gently fold the whipped cream into the gelatin mixture along with the drained fruit cocktail. Refrigerate for another 5-10 minutes.

9. Transfer the mixture into the prepared pie shell.
10. Refrigerate the pie for 2-4 hours. If desired, top the dish with any leftover fruit before serving.

Nutrition (per serving)
Calories 268, fat 18 g, carbs 23 g, sugar 6 g,
Protein 4 g, sodium 51 mg

Eggnog Chiffon Pie

This 1940s recipe came from an old dairy company according to my aunt Eunice's recipe notes. Eggnog lovers will surely find this a wonderfully creamy and rich dessert, perfect for the holidays. She used to add a touch of rum in her eggnog!

Serves 8 | Prep. time 40 minutes | Chill time 2 hours

Ingredients

1 shortcrust pie shell, prebaked
1 envelope unflavored gelatin
¼ cup cold water
1¾ cup eggnog
2 teaspoons cornstarch
2 tablespoons rum flavoring or the real thing
½ cup heavy cream, whipped stiff
3 egg whites
¼ teaspoon cream of tartar
6 tablespoons sugar
Nutmeg, to taste
⅓ cup crushed graham cracker mixed with 4 tablespoons coarsely chopped pecans
Whipped cream for topping, if desired

Directions

1. In a bowl, soak gelatin in cold water.
2. In a saucepan over medium heat, mix eggnog and cornstarch. Once it boils, let it simmer for 5-10 minutes until it thickens. Remove from it and add the gelatin. Let it cool.

3. When the mixture sets, using an electric mixer, beat until it becomes smooth.
4. Add rum flavoring and fold in the whipped cream gently.
5. In another bowl, combine egg whites and cream of tartar. Beat until the mixture becomes foamy.
6. Gradually add sugar and beat until it becomes stiff.
7. Add the rum mixture to the meringue. Fold together until well incorporated.
8. Spread the filling onto the prebaked pie crust. Sprinkle with nutmeg then chill for 2 hours or until set.
9. Twenty minutes before serving, remove from the refrigerator and ring the crust with the graham and pecan mixture.
10. Top with whipped cream and serve.

Nutrition (per serving)
Calories 268, fat 15 g, carbs 28 g, sugar 16 g,
Protein 7 g, sodium 148 mg

Funeral Pie

This pie is rich with autumn flavors, such as allspice and cinnamon. It was a popular to bring during wakes at funeral by the early settlers. It originally came with German settlers and is also known as Rosina Pie.

Serves 10 | Prep. time 15 minutes | Cooking time 40 minutes

Ingredients
1 double-crust pie shells
2 cups raisins
1 cup water
1 cup orange juice
½ cup packed light brown sugar
½ cup granulated sugar
3 tablespoons corn starch
1½ teaspoons ground cinnamon
½ teaspoon allspice
1 cup chopped walnuts
1 pinch kosher salt
1 tablespoon apple cider vinegar
3 tablespoons unsalted butter
1 large egg, beaten well

Directions

1. Preheat the oven to 400°F (204°C).
2. In a large saucepan, add the water, orange juice, and raisins. Cook for 5 minutes on medium heat, or until the raisins are plump.
3. Meanwhile, in a small mixing bowl, whisk together both sugars, corn starch, cinnamon, and allspice.
4. Add the sugar mixture to the orange juice mixture. Cook and stir for 5 minutes, or until the mixture thickens and

bubbles.
5. Take off the heat and add the walnuts, butter, and vinegar. Combine well.
6. Transfer the pie crust with the mixture, then top with the second crust, firmly crimping the edges.
7. Using a knife, slit the top crust to allow steam to escape, then brush lightly with the beaten egg.
8. Bake for 25-30 minutes, or until the crust is golden-brown.
9. Cool the pie completely on a wire rack before serving.

Nutrition (per serving)
Calories 465, fat 17 g, carbs 76 g, sugar 54 g,
Protein 4 g, sodium 550 mg

Marlborough Pie

The creation of the Marlborough pie is traced back to 1660 in the UK. It was introduced to America during the 17th century as a special treat to celebrate the harvest and has been shared during Thanksgiving meals ever since.

Serves 8 | Prep time 10 minutes
Cooling time 4 hours | Cook time 1 hour

Ingredients
1 (9-inch) pie crust, baked
4 tablespoons butter
4 cups apple, peeled and shredded (combine Granny Smith Apples with sweeter varieties)
½ cup sugar
¼ teaspoon cinnamon
¼ teaspoon nutmeg
¼ teaspoon salt
3 eggs, lightly beaten
½ cup heavy cream
5 tablespoons dry sherry
1 teaspoon grated lemon zest
1 teaspoon vanilla extract
Whipped cream, as garnish

Directions

1. Preheat the oven to 325°F (163°C).
2. Melt the butter in a skillet over medium heat.
3. Add the shredded apples and cook, stirring frequently, for 15 minutes. The mixture should be very dry, with almost all the liquid evaporated.
4. Let it cool.

5. Combine the sugar, cinnamon, nutmeg, and salt in a large bowl.
6. Whisk in the eggs, cream, sherry, lemon zest, and vanilla, and mix until smooth.
7. Stir in the apples and transfer the mixture to a pie shell.
8. Bake until set (about 40 minutes).
9. Remove the pie from the oven and set it on a rack. Let cool for about 4 hours.
10. Chill, and serve with whipped cream.

Nutrition (per serving)
Calories 347, fat 21 g, carbs 35 g, sugar 19 g,
Protein 4 g, sodium 219 mg

Soda Cracker Pie

This old Carolina pie is a testament to Southerners' resourcefulness since this is one of the many desperation pies, or "make-do pies" which were recipes made to cope with the limited ingredients such as butter and flour and dwindling supplies during World War II. Yet until now, this pie has stood the test of time and is loved by many households, especially during the holidays or as a sweet ending to a barbecue party.

Serves 8 | Prep. time 10 minutes | Cooking time 20 minutes

Ingredients

18 soda crackers, also known as saltine crackers
1 cup pecans, chopped
3 eggs whites
1 cup white sugar
1 teaspoon vanilla extract
1 teaspoon baking powder
⅛ teaspoon cream of tartar
6 ripe peaches, cored, peeled, and sliced
Whipped cream for topping

Directions

1. Preheat oven to 350°F (191°C). Grease a 9-inch pie dish.
2. Place the crackers in a sealable bag. With a roll pin, crush the crackers. Placed the crushed crackers into a large mixing bowl, and add pecans and baking powder. Combine well, and set aside.
3. Place the egg whites into a mixing bowl, and add the cream of tartar. Beat the egg whites on high speed until

you get stiff picks. Slowly add the sugar and the vanilla while continuously beating until well combined.
4. Add the egg whites to the dry mixture. Stir with a wooden spoon or spatula just enough to combine.
5. Pour the mixture into the pie dish, and bake 23-25 minutes, until golden. Remove from oven, and let cool on a wired rack.
6. To serve, cut into slices, top with peach slices and whipped cream.

Nutrition (per serving)
Calories 255, fat 11 g, carbs 36 g, sugar 28 g,
Protein 6 g, sodium 171 mg

NUT AND DRIED FRUIT-BASED PIES

Mom's Pecan Pie

A favorite in every state in the South, this pecan pie with its sweet pecan filling and the delicious crust will be a perfect ending to every any meal. The origins of the pecan pie are quite unclear but most probably it was created by French settlers to Louisiana discovering pecans nuts for the first time. This recipe is my mom's recipe which I make often because it's that good. She added maple syrup, and this makes so much more flavorful.

Serves 8 | Prep. time 10 minutes | Cooking time 50 to 55 minutes

Ingredients
1 (9-inch) plain pastry pie shell
½ cup corn syrup
½ cup maple syrup
1 cup sugar
3 large eggs, lightly beaten
¼ teaspoon salt
2 tablespoons unsalted butter, melted
1 teaspoon vanilla
2 cups pecans, halved

Directions

1. Preheat the oven to 350°F (177°C).
2. Warm the corn syrup over a double boiler to make it pourable.
3. Pour the syrup into a bowl along with the honey, sugar, eggs, salt, melted butter, and vanilla. Mix or whisk well.

4. Arrange the pecans in your pastry-lined pie plate and pour the syrup over them.
5. Place the pie plate on a baking tray to catch any drips and bake until golden brown (about 50-55 minutes).

Nutrition (per serving)
Calories 541, fat 28 g, carbs 73 g, sugar 60 g,
Protein 6 g, sodium 218 mg

Old-Fashioned Pecan Pie

This was one of my grandmother's favorite pecan pie recipes. The use of dark corn syrup gives it a darker color and so much sweetness. This pie will surely catch everyone's eye and become an instant favorite at every dinner party.

Serves 8 | Prep. time 10 minutes | Cooking time 40 minutes

Ingredients
1 (9-inch) pie shell
1 cup pecans

Filling
3 eggs
⅔ cup sugar
⅓ teaspoon salt
⅓ cup butter, melted
1 cup dark corn syrup

Directions

1. Preheat the oven to 375°F (191°C).
2. Arrange pecans on the bottom surface of the pie.
3. In a bowl, beat the filling ingredients together. Pour over the pecans.
4. Bake for 40-50 minutes.

Nutrition (per serving)
Calories 453, fat 23 g, carbs 62 g, sugar 51 g,
Protein 4 g, sodium 272 mg

Caramel Pecan Pie

This pie was first invented in the 1960s. It contains a pudding filling of pecans, caramel candies, and gelatin.

Serves 8 | Prep. time 15 minutes
Cooking time 5-10 minutes | Chill time 40-45 minutes

Ingredients
1 (9-inch) graham cracker crust
1 envelope gelatin, unflavored
¼ cup cold water
½ pound caramel candies
¾ cup whole milk
¼ teaspoon kosher salt
1 cup heavy cream, whipped
½ cup chopped pecans

Directions

1. Soak the gelatin in cold water to soften it. Set aside.
2. Combine the caramel candies and milk on top of a double boiler. Stirring occasionally, heat over boiling water until melted.
3. Turn off the heat and stir in the salt and dissolved gelatin.
4. Refrigerate until partially set.
5. Transfer into the prepared crust. Arrange the whipped cream and pecans over the filling.
6. Refrigerate until fully set, at least 30 minutes, before serving.

Nutrition (per serving)
Calories 535, fat 28 g, carbs 66 g, sugar 49 g,
Protein 7 g, sodium 371.2 mg

Bourbon Pecan Pie

The pecan pie was invented in the 1890s and made its way to Thanksgiving tables, earning a spot right alongside pumpkin pie. This recipe takes more of a southern twist and uses the flavor of bourbon to make it extra special.

Serves 8 | Prep. time 20 minutes
Chilling time 1 hour | Cooking time 1 hour 10 minutes

Ingredients

For the crust
1½ cups all-purpose flour
¼ teaspoon baking soda
½ teaspoon salt
6 tablespoons butter, cubed and well chilled
¼ cup vegetable shortening
¼ cup ice water

For the pie filling
¼ cup + 2 tablespoons butter, melted and browned
⅔ cup dark brown sugar
1⅔ cups corn syrup
3 eggs
¼ cup high-quality bourbon
1 teaspoon pure vanilla extract
½ teaspoon salt
1½ cups pecans, chopped
1½ cups pecans, whole
Whipped cream for garnish, optional

Directions

1. To make the crust, combine the flour, baking soda, and salt in a large bowl or food processor and mix.

2. Cut in the butter and vegetable shortening until crumbly.
3. Add the water and mix just until a dough forms.
4. Transfer to a lightly floured surface, roll into a ball, and flatten it slightly. Cover in plastic wrap and chill for one hour.
5. Preheat the oven to 400°F (204°C).
6. Remove the crust from the refrigerator and lightly flour a work surface.
7. Place the crust on the work surface and roll it out into a circle large enough for a (9-inch) pie dish.
8. Lift the crust from the counter and drape it over the pie dish, crimping the edges with your fingers or a fork.
9. Line the bottom of the crust with parchment paper and place a layer of dried beans or baking weights inside.
10. Bake for 20 minutes, or until lightly golden brown.
11. Remove the pie crust from the oven, lift out the weights and parchment paper, and reduce the temperature of the oven to 350°F (177°C).
12. To make the filling, place the melted butter in a bowl along with the brown sugar, corn syrup, eggs, bourbon, vanilla extract, and salt. Whisk until well blended and creamy.
13. Place the chopped pecans in the pie crust. Pour the filling over the chopped pecans and then arrange the whole pecans on top.
14. Bake for 50 minutes.
15. Remove from the oven and let it sit and let cool completely. The pie will continue to cook as it cools, so don't cut into it right away.
16. Serve with whipped cream, if desired.

Nutrition (per serving)
Calories 836, fat 51 g, carbs 92 g, sugar 70 g,
Protein 9 g, sodium 282 mg

Kentucky Derby Pie

This retro, gooey pie is made with chocolate chips and pecans.

Serves 10 | Prep. time 25 minutes | Cooking time 55 minutes

Ingredients
2 (9-inch) pie shells, frozen
4 large eggs
½ cup granulated sugar
½ cup light brown sugar
1 cup semi-sweet chocolate chips
6 ounces pecans, halved
1 cup corn syrup
1 stick unsalted butter, melted
1 teaspoon pure vanilla extract
¼ teaspoon kosher salt

Directions

1. Preheat the oven to 350°F (177°C).
2. In a medium mixing bowl, microwave the butter until melted.
3. Using a hand mixer, beat together the eggs, corn syrup, sugar, vanilla, and salt in a large mixing bowl.
4. Add the melted butter to the egg mixture and mix until well combined.
5. Divide the pecans and chocolate chips into each pie shell. Then, divide the filling mixture between each pie shell.
6. Bake for about 45 minutes.
7. To avoid the crust edges from over-crisping, transfer the pies to the bottom rack of the oven halfway through.
8. If the pies are not finished, bake for another 10 minutes.
9. Let cool before serving.

Nutrition (per serving)
Calories 540, fat 32 g, carbs 59 g, sugar 33 g, Protein 5 g, sodium 180 mg

Praline Pie

This praline pie, first invented in 1970, is made with pecan and pudding in a crunchy pie shell.

Serves 8 | Prep. time 15 minutes
Cooking time 10 minutes | Chill time 30 minutes

Ingredients
1 (9-inch) pie shell, baked and cooled
⅓ cup unsalted butter
⅓ cup firmly packed dark brown sugar
½ cup chopped pecans
1 (5-ounce) package Jell-O vanilla pudding and pie filling
3 cups whole milk
1 envelope Dream Whip topping mix

Directions

1. Preheat the oven to 450°F (232°C).
2. In a small saucepan, melt the butter, brown sugar, and nuts over medium heat.
3. Spread the mixture across the pie crust's base. Bake for 5 minutes.
4. Transfer the pie to a wire rack and cool.
5. In the meantime, prepare the Jell-O pie filling mix with milk as directed on the package. Cool for 5 minutes.
6. Take out 1 cup of the filling, wrap it in wax paper, and refrigerate until chilled, at least 30 minutes. Transfer the remaining filling to the pie shell and refrigerate as well for 30 minutes.
7. Prepare the whipped topping mix per package instructions.
8. In a medium mixing bowl, gently fold 1⅓ cups of the topping into the chilled pie filling.

9. Spread the pie filling in the pie shell over the previous layer of filling.
10. If desired, top with the pecans and remaining whipped topping.
11. Serve immediately.

Nutrition (per serving)
Calories 429, fat 26 g, carbs 44 g, sugar 33 g,
Protein 4 g, sodium 455 mg

Bakewell Tart

Served warm with cream or even cool with a cup of tea, this fragrant tart will surely make you fall in love with the combination of raspberry and almonds.

Serves 8 | Prep. time 45 minutes
Chilling time 7 hours | Cooking time 1 hour

Ingredients

For the dough
½ cup butter, room temperature
⅔ cup icing sugar, sifted
2 cups flour, sifted
2 large eggs

¼ cup raspberry jam

For the filling
¾ cup butter, room temperature
¾ cup sugar
3 eggs
3 tablespoons flour
1 ¾ cups almond flour
1 teaspoon almond extract
¼ cup sliced almonds

Directions

1. Combine the butter and icing sugar and beat until smooth. Mix in one egg and about ¾ cup of flour. Continue mixing and adding flour gradually until a dough forms. Do not overmix.
2. Wrap and refrigerate the dough for 6 hours.

3. Thirty minutes before continuing, remove the dough from the fridge.
4. Dust a clean work surface with flour and roll the dough to a ¼-inch thickness for a 10-inch tart pan. Trim the edges and reserve the extra dough.
5. Prick the bottom of the pie and refrigerate for 1 hour.
6. Preheat the oven to 375°F (191°C). Cover the dough with parchment and fill it with dry beans. Bake for 15 minutes.
7. Remove the crust from the oven and take out the beans and parchment. Use the leftover dough to fill any cracks.
8. Beat the remaining egg and brush it over the whole inside of the crust.
9. Return the crust to the oven and bake for 5 minutes, until lightly golden.
10. When the shell has cooled completely, spread the jam in it.
11. Preheat the oven to 350°F (177°C).
12. Make the frangipane filling. Beat the butter with the sugar until the mixture becomes white and firm. Mix in the eggs one at a time, then the flour, almond flour, and extract.
13. Spread the filling over the jam, being careful not to disturb the jam. Sprinkle the sliced almonds on top.
14. Bake for 45 minutes. Cool completely before slicing.

Nutrition (per serving)
Calories 691, fat 43 g, carbs 68 g, sugar 36 g,
Protein 13 g, sodium 50 mg

Raisin Pie

Prepare this delightfully great and refreshingly tasty pie for your family. You will surely receive huge appreciation from all. I grew up on raisin pie. It was a budget-friendly pie in the 60s and 70s.

Serves 8 | Prep. time 15 minutes | Cooking time 45 minutes

Ingredients
2 (9-inch) pie shells
2 cups water
½ cup sugar
2 tablespoons flour
¼ teaspoon salt
½ teaspoon vanilla extract
1 tablespoon butter
1 tablespoon freshly squeezed lemon juice
2 cups raisins

Directions

1. Preheat the oven to 450°F (232°C) and prepare a pie plate with a bottom crust of pastry.
2. In a large saucepan, mix the water, sugar, flour, salt, vanilla, butter, and lemon juice together.
3. Stir in the raisins.
4. Bring the mixture to a simmer and cook over low heat for 10 minutes, stirring frequently.
5. Pour the filling into the pastry-lined pie pan.
6. Cover with the top pastry. Trim and flute the edges and make slits on top as vents.
7. Bake for 15 minutes, then reduce the heat to 350°F (177°C) and bake 25-30 minutes longer.

Nutrition (per serving)

Calories 361, fat 12 g, carbs 66 g, sugar 37 g, Protein 4 g, sodium 249 mg

Kool Aid Pie

This vintage pie tastes like Kool-Aid, and it's made with only four ingredients!

Serves 8 | Prep. time 5-10 minutes | Chill time 4 hours

Ingredients
1 graham-cracker pie crust, premade
1 (14-ounce) can sweetened condensed milk
1 packet unsweetened Kool-Aid, any flavor
1 (8-ounce) tub Cool Whip

Directions

1. Add the condensed milk to a medium mixing bowl.
2. Add the packet of Kool-Aid and stir to combine.
3. Add the Cool Whip and mix until well-combined.
4. Fill the prepared pie crust with the mixture.
5. Cover and refrigerate for at least 4 hours, then serve.

Nutrition (per serving)
Calories 389, fat 16 g, carbs 53 g, sugar 42 g,
Protein 5 g, sodium 234 mg

Hillbilly Pie

Similar to the Oatmeal pie, this old recipe from the Ozarks is so easy to prepare with fewer ingredients and the kids love to help me make it!

Serves 8 | Prep. time 15 minutes | Cooking time 1 hour

Ingredients
1 (9-inch) pie crust, unbaked
1 (8-ounce) package cream cheese, softened
⅓ cup granulated sugar
2 tablespoons pure vanilla extract, divided
3 large eggs, beaten
1 cup corn syrup
1 cup dark brown sugar, packed
2 tablespoons unsalted butter, softened
1 tablespoon all-purpose flour
1 tablespoon pure vanilla extract
1½ cups rolled oats

Directions

1. Preheat the oven to 350°F (177°C).
2. In a medium mixing bowl, combine the cream cheese, sugar, and 1 tablespoon of vanilla extract.
3. Pour the mixture into the pie crust.
4. In another medium bowl, combine the eggs, corn syrup, brown sugar, butter, flour, and the remaining 1 tablespoon of vanilla extract together.
5. Fold in the rolled oats until well-combined.
6. Pour the mixture over the cream cheese layer in the pie crust.
7. Bake for 1 hour or until the center has set.
8. Let the pie cool, then serve immediately.

Nutrition (per serving)
Calories 583, fat 22 g, carbs 89 g, sugar 46 g, Protein 7 g, sodium 277.7 mg

Shoofly Pie

Originating for the 1890s, the shoofly pie gained popularity in the 1960s and once you take one bite off this pie, you'll know why.

Serves 8 | Prep. time 15 minutes | Cooking time 35 minutes

Ingredients
1 (9-inch) pie shell

For the filling
½ teaspoon baking soda
¾ cup boiling water
1 cup dark molasses
½ cup brown sugar
1½ cups flour
¼ cup shortening or butter

Directions

1. Preheat the oven to 375°F (191°C).
2. In a bowl, combine the baking soda, hot water, and molasses.
3. In another bowl, combine the sugar and flour. Rub in the shortening until the mixture looks like crumbs.
4. Pour ⅓ of the molasses mixture into the pie shell and follow with ⅓ of the crumb mixture.
5. Repeat the layers, making sure to end with the crumb mixture on top.
6. Bake for 35 minutes.

Nutrition (per serving)
Calories 395, fat 12 g, carbs 66 g, sugar 39 g,
Protein 4 g, sodium 105 mg

APPLE-BASED PIES
Apple Cheddar Pie

Apple pie is a classic American dessert, no matter what time of year. In the 1980s, we got wise to the idea of how well apple and cheddar go together and finally got around to blending them in a pie. Take a trip back in time with this one. It's worth it.

Serves 8 | Prep. time 30 minutes
Cooking time 50 minutes | Chilling time 4 hours+

Ingredients
For the crust
2½ cups all-purpose flour
1 tablespoon white sugar
1 teaspoon salt
1 cup cold butter, cubed
½ cup ice water
1 cup good quality, medium sharp cheddar cheese, shredded
Vanilla ice cream to serve

For the filling
12 cups baking apples, peeled and sliced
½ cup white sugar
3 tablespoons all-purpose flour
2 teaspoons cinnamon
½ teaspoon ground ginger
½ teaspoon nutmeg
½ cup cheddar cheese, shredded

Directions

1. For the pie crust, combine the flour, sugar, and salt in a bowl or in a stand mixer. Mix until blended.

2. Cut in the cubed butter, mixing until the dough is crumbly.
3. Add the cold water a couple of teaspoons at a time, mixing until you have a good dough consistency.
4. Transfer the dough out onto a floured surface.
5. Add the cheddar cheese to the dough and work it in with your hands.
6. Cover the dough in plastic wrap and refrigerate for at least an hour.
7. Remove the dough from the refrigerator and divide the dough in half. Roll it out into two circles that are approximately 12 inches in diameter.
8. Place one pie crust in the pie dish, making sure that it's pressed down against the bottom and sides.
9. Meanwhile, preheat the oven to 400°F (204°C).
10. In a bowl, combine the apple slices, white sugar, flour, cinnamon, ginger, nutmeg, and cheddar cheese. Toss to mix well.
11. Transfer the fruit mixture to the pie dish.
12. Place the second pie crust over the fruit.
13. Crimp the sides of the pie crust, sealing the top and bottom crusts together.
14. Make decorative slices on the top crust to allow for steam venting during cooking.
15. Place the pie dish in the center of the oven and bake for 25 minutes.
16. Reduce the heat to 375°F (191°C) and cook for an additional 25–30 minutes.
17. Remove the pie from the oven and set it aside to cool for several hours. This allows the apples to continue cooking and lets the liquid thicken a bit inside the pie.
18. Serve with a scoop of vanilla ice cream if desired.

Nutrition (per serving)
Calories 582, fat 30 g, carbs 72 g, sugar 33 g,

Protein 10 g, sodium 435 mg

Apple Scottish Pie

This pie was first invented in Scotland, hence its name. Unlike its American counterpart, this pie has gingersnap cookies, raisins, and marmalade.

Serves 8 | Prep. time 30 minutes | Cooking time 50-55 minutes

Ingredients
2 (15-ounce) plain pastry pie crusts, room temperature
1½ pounds Granny Smith apples, peeled, cored, cut into small cubes
9 tablespoons granulated sugar, divided
½ cup gingersnap cookie crumbs
⅓ cup orange marmalade
⅓ cup golden raisins
1 teaspoon orange zest
1 tablespoon heavy whipping cream

Directions

1. Preheat the oven to 375°F (191°C).
2. Prepare 1 pie crust in a (9-inch) diameter glass pie dish.
3. In a large mixing bowl, combine the apples, 8 tablespoons of sugar, gingersnap cookie crumbs, marmalade, raisins, and orange zest.
4. Spoon the filling into the prepared pie dish. Top with the remaining pie crust.
5. Seal the crust edges by pressing them together, crimping the edges if desired.
6. With a knife, make a 1-inch hole in the center of the pie.
7. In a small mixing bowl, add the whipping cream and the remaining 1 tablespoon of sugar. Mix to combine, and then brush over the pie crust.

8. Bake for 45-50 minutes, or until the pie crust is golden-brown and the filling is bubbling.
9. Serve immediately.

Nutrition (per serving)
Calories 221, fat 3 g, carbs 48 g, sugar 32 g,
Protein 1 g, sodium 146 mg

Apple Crumble Pie

This pie has a classic caramel apple flavor that is dense, rich, and soft. Crumble pies were so popular in the 60s and 70s.

Serves 10 | Prep. time 5 minutes | Cooking time 50-60 minutes

Ingredients
1 (9-inch) pie crust, frozen
¼ cup unsalted butter, melted
1 large egg
¾ cup granulated sugar
¼ cup light brown sugar
1½ teaspoons pure vanilla extract
1 teaspoon ground cinnamon
¼ teaspoon allspice
¼ teaspoon ground cloves
¼ teaspoon kosher salt, optional
¾ cup all-purpose flour
¾ cup whole rolled old-fashioned oats (not instant or quick-cooking)
1 (21-ounce) can apple pie filling
Caramel sauce or caramel ice cream, for topping
Whipped cream, for topping

Directions

1. Preheat the oven to 350°F (177°C).
2. In a large, microwave-safe bowl, microwave the butter on high for 1 minute.
3. Let the butter cool for a moment. Add the egg, both sugars, vanilla extract, cinnamon, allspice, cloves, and salt (if using).
4. Add the flour and oats and combine.
5. Add the apple pie filling and whisk until well-combined.

6. Transfer the filling mixture into the prepared crust. Smooth the filling on the top of the pie with a spatula.
7. Transfer the pie crust to a baking sheet to prevent it from pooling in the oven's bottom.
8. Bake for 50 to 60 minutes, or until golden-brown.
9. Before slicing and serving, cool the pie for at least 30 minutes. Before serving, drizzle with the caramel sauce or serve with caramel ice cream.

Nutrition (per serving)
Calories 356, fat 12 g, carbs 61 g, sugar 40 g,
Protein 4 g, sodium 201 mg

Norwegian Apple Pie

This apple pie became popular during the 1970s in America and as its name suggest, it originated in Norway long before. This simple yet flavor-packed pie is perfect to prepare this weekend and relive a classic taste of the 70s.

Serves 4 | Prep. time 10 minutes | Cooking time 30 minutes

Ingredients
1 egg
¾ cup sugar
1 teaspoon vanilla
¼ teaspoon salt
1 teaspoon baking powder
½ cup flour
½ cup nuts, chopped
1 cup apples, diced

Directions

1. Preheat the oven to 350°F (177°C).
2. Beat the eggs in a mixing bowl. Mix in the sugar and vanilla.
3. In another mixing bowl, mix the salt, flour, and baking powder.
4. Combine both the mixtures and mix well.
5. Mix in the nuts and apples.
6. Grease an 8-inch pie pan with some butter or cooking oil.
7. Pour the batter into the pan. Bake for about 30 minutes until the top is golden brown.
8. Slice and serve warm.

Nutrition (per serving)
Calories 328, fat 9 g, carbs 56 g, sugar 40 g,

Protein 7 g, sodium 326 mg

Johnny Appleseed Pie

This pie hit the scene in the 1970s. Made with apples and maple syrup, this pie is as American as they come.

Serves 8 | Prep. time 25 minutes | Cooking time 50 minutes

Ingredients
1 (9-inch) plain pastry pie shell
¼ cup + 2 tablespoons maple syrup, divided
½ cup granulated sugar
2 tablespoons quick-cooking tapioca
1 tablespoon lemon juice
1 teaspoon ground cinnamon
½ teaspoon ground nutmeg
¼ teaspoon kosher salt
2 tablespoons unsalted butter
6 cups apples, peeled, cored, and sliced

Directions

1. Preheat the oven to 450°F (232°C).
2. In a large mixing bowl, combine ¼ cup maple syrup, sugar, tapioca, lemon juice, cinnamon, nutmeg, and salt.
3. Add apples and stir to combine.
4. Line a well-greased (9-inch) pie pan with the pastry.
5. Add apple mixture to the bottom of the crust, then dot with the butter.
6. Arrange the top crust over the filling, pressing, and crimping the edges together.
7. Use a knife to cut slits on top of the pie.
8. Bake for 40 minutes or until the crust is golden-brown.
9. Glaze the top crust with 2 tablespoons of maple syrup and bake for another 10 minutes.
10. Let the pie cool somewhat before serving.

Nutrition (per serving)
Calories 218, fat 4 g, carbs 47 g, sugar 34 g, Protein 1 g, sodium 139 mg

King Kamehameha Pie

This 1970s-era pie invented is glazed with pineapple juice and contains sweet apple chunks.

Serves 8 | Prep. time 30 minutes | Cooking time 30 minutes

Ingredients
1 (9-inch) pie shell, baked and cooled
1½ cups pineapple juice, divided
¾ cup granulated sugar
7 cups medium yellow apples, peeled, cored, and cut into wedges
3 tablespoons corn starch
1 tablespoon unsalted butter
½ teaspoon pure vanilla extract
¼ teaspoon kosher salt

Directions

1. In a large saucepan, combine 1¼ cups pineapple juice and the sugar.
2. Bring to a boil over medium-high heat.
3. Add the apple wedges and cover. Simmer for 3-4 minutes. Apples should be fork-tender but not soft.
4. Drain apples out of the syrup. In a small mixing bowl, combine the remaining pineapple juice with the corn starch, and add them to the saucepan.
5. Cook, stirring constantly until the sauce thickens and bubbles. Then, cook for 1 more minute.
6. Take the saucepan off the heat and add the salt, vanilla extract, and butter. Let cool for 10 minutes without stirring.
7. Spread half the syrup over the bottom of the baked pie shell.
8. Top with the cooked apples. Drizzle the remaining syrup over the apples.

9. Let it cool to room temperature or refrigerate for at least 30 minutes if you want to serve it chilled.
10. If desired, put a dollop of whipped cream or sour cream on the pie's center as a garnish. Top with chopped macadamia nuts if desired, then serve.

Nutrition (per serving)
Calories 242, fat 4 g, carbs 53 g, sugar 38 g,
Protein 2 g, sodium 112 mg

Candy Apple Pie

This classic pie gives you a beautiful golden pie crust with sweet tender apples.

Serves 8 | Prep. time 20 minutes | Cooking time 30 minutes

Ingredients
3 large Granny Smith apples, cored and peeled
¼ cup granulated sugar
1 cup all-purpose flour
1 cup packed light brown sugar
¼ teaspoon kosher salt
½ teaspoon ground cinnamon
Dash ground nutmeg
½ cup salted butter, diced into cubes
Caramel sauce, for serving
Vanilla ice cream, for serving

Directions

1. Preheat the oven to 350°F (177°C).
2. Slice the apples into ¼- to ½-inch thick pieces (depending on how tender you want the apples after baking).
3. Use non-stick cooking spray to lightly grease a (9-inch) pie plate.
4. On the pie plate, layer half the sliced apples and garnish with sugar.
5. On top of the first apple layer, arrange the remaining sliced applies.
6. In a food processor, add the flour, brown sugar, salt, cinnamon, and nutmeg. Add the cubed butter in small batches and pulse until the mixture resembles coarse crumbs.
7. On top of the pie, evenly distribute the flour mixture.

8. Bake for about 30 minutes or until golden brown.
9. Let the pie cool for 15 minutes before slicing. Serve it with ice cream and caramel sauce.

Nutrition (per serving)
Calories 331, fat 12 g, carbs 57 g, sugar 42 g,
Protein 2 g, sodium 183 mg

Apple Butter Hand Pies

My aunt Eunice would make these pies in the fall during the apple season. They made the whole house smell so good. Make the apple butter the day before as it takes quite some time to cook in a slow cooker. You can also can it and freeze but usually, it`s gone by the end of the week!

Serves 20 | Prep time 30 minutes
Cooking time 10 hours and 15-20 minutes

Ingredients
For the apple butter filling (makes about 8 cups)
6 pounds red cooking apples
½ cup sugar
½ cup packed dark brown sugar
1 tablespoon cinnamon or to taste
2 teaspoons pure vanilla extract
¼ teaspoon salt

For the pie
½ cup unsalted butter
½ cup shortening
3 ½ cups all-purpose flour
1 teaspoon kosher salt
3 tablespoons granulated sugar
2 large eggs, room temperature, and divided
½ tablespoon apple cider vinegar
½ cup water

Directions

1. Make the apple butter first. In a slow cooker, add all the ingredients. Stir to mix well. Set on LOW for 8-10 hours taking care of stirring 1-2 times each hour. The color

should turn dark brown. After the apple butter is well cooked, using a blender stick, blend until smooth. Set aside and let cool completely before storing in airtight containers such as canning jars in the refrigerator. It will keep for 3 weeks in the fridge and up to 3 months in the freezer.
2. Preheat oven to 350°F (177°C). Line a baking sheet with parchment paper.
3. In a large mixing bowl, combine the flour, sugar, and salt.
4. Stir the butter and shortening into the mixture. Combine all the ingredients until crumbly.
5. Add 1 egg and apple cider vinegar. Combine well.
6. Using your hands, form a smooth dough from the mixture.
7. Roll out the dough on a lightly floured working surface. Cut 5-inch circles from the dough with a glass or a cookie cutter.
8. Add a teaspoon or two of the apple butter filling to the center of each dough circle. Close to the mini pies. Seal the edges using a fork.
9. Beat the remaining egg in a small bowl.
10. Arrange the mini pies on the prepared baking sheet. Brush them with the beaten egg and sprinkle brown sugar on top if desired.
11. Bake for about 15-20 minutes. Serve warm.

Nutrition (per serving)
Calories 184, fat 11 g, carbs 18.5 g, sugar 1.9 g,
Protein 2.9 g, sodium 157 mg

BERRY PIES

Blueberry Pie

The fresh blueberries give this pie a naturally sweet flavor that pairs beautifully with the flaky pie crust.

Serves 8 | Prep. time 15 minutes | Cooking time 1 hour 10 minutes

Ingredients

For the crust
2 cups all-purpose flour, plus more for rolling the crust
½ teaspoon kosher salt
⅔ cup shortening
4 ½ tablespoons ice-cold water, or more as needed
1 tablespoon whole milk, for garnish
Granulated sugar or cinnamon sugar, for garnish
1 tablespoon unsalted butter, melted, for garnish

For the filling
6 cups fresh blueberries, rinsed and drained, divided
½ cup granulated sugar
⅓ cup water
4 tablespoons corn starch
Pinch of kosher salt
2 teaspoons lemon juice
Pinch of ground cinnamon (optional)

Directions

1. Preheat oven to 350°F (177°C).
2. Grease the bottom and sides of a (9-inch) pie plate with cooking spray.
3. To make the filling, heat a large saucepan over medium heat. Add the sugar, corn starch, water, and salt until well-

combined.
4. Add 4 cups of the blueberries. Bring to a boil and simmer until thickened.
5. Remove the saucepan from the heat, then stir in the lemon juice and cinnamon.
6. Add the remaining 2 cups of blueberries and stir until well combined.
7. Prior to filling the pie crust, allow the filling to cool slightly.
8. In the meantime, to prepare the crust, add the flour, shortening, and salt to a large mixing bowl. Mix together with a pastry cutter or fork until the mixture resembles coarse crumbles.
9. Taking care not to overwork the dough, slowly incorporate the water until a ball of dough forms.
10. On a lightly floured surface, roll out the dough into 2 12-inch rounds. The rounds should be roughly ⅛-inch thick for the bottom and top of a round (9-inch) pie plate.
11. Add the bottom round to the prepared pie plate, then add the filling. Add the top crust to cover the filling.
12. Using your fingers or the tines of a fork, pinch the dough edges together to create a decorative border.
13. Using a fork or knife, poke the pie's top crust.
14. Top the pie with the cinnamon-sugar mixture, granulated sugar, drops of milk, and melted butter.
15. Bake for 45-55 minutes, or until the crust is golden-brown and the filling is bubbling. If the crust starts to brown too quickly on the edges, wrap the edges with foil.
16. Serve warm or cool.

Nutrition (per serving)
Calories 364, fat 24 g, carbs 38 g, sugar 31 g
Protein 1 g, sodium 625 mg

Maine's Settler Blueberry Pie

This pie goes way back to the 18th century! It contains fresh blueberries, vinegar, and sugar.

Serves 8 | Prep. time 15-20 minutes
Cooking time 25-30 minutes | Chill time 4 hours 30 minutes

Ingredients
1 (9-inch) plain pastry pie shell
3 tablespoons all-purpose flour
¼ teaspoon salt
1 cup water, divided
¾ cup granulated sugar
6 cups fresh blueberries, divided
½ teaspoon white vinegar
Sweetened whipped cream or vanilla ice cream, for serving

Directions

1. Preheat oven to 425°F (218°C).
2. On a lightly floured surface, roll out the pie crust to a circle that is ⅛ inch thick. Transfer it to a (9-inch) pie dish.
3. Flute the crust edges and trim to ½ inch beyond the dish's rim.
4. Refrigerate for 30 minutes. Use 2 layers of aluminum foil to line the crust.
5. Place pie weights, uncooked rice, or dry beans on the foil.
6. Bake on the lower oven rack for 20 to 25 minutes.
7. Remove the foil and weights, then bake for another 3-6 minutes or until the crust is golden-brown. Transfer the pie to a wire rack to cool completely.
8. In a small mixing bowl, combine the flour, salt, and ⅓ cup of water.

9. In a large saucepan, add the remaining water, 1 cup of blueberries, and the sugar. Bring to a boil. Add the flour mixture and stir thoroughly.
10. Boil for 4-6 minutes, stirring constantly, until thickened,
11. Transfer the mixture into the crust. Drizzle it with vinegar and top with any remaining blueberries.
12. Refrigerate the pie for at least 4 hours. Top with whipped cream before serving.

Nutrition (per serving)
Calories 307, fat 12 g, carbs 49 g, sugar 28 g,
Protein 3 g, sodium 230 mg

Creamy Blue Pie

This pie, first made in the 1960s, has a delightfully creamy texture with blueberry flavors.

Serves 8 | Prep. time 5-10 minutes
Cooking time 5 minutes | Chill time 3-4 hours

Ingredients
1 (9-inch) graham cracker crust
¼ cup cold water
1 envelope gelatin, unflavored
1 (14-ounce) can sweetened condensed milk
⅓ cup lemon juice
½ pint sour cream
2 ½ cups blueberry pie filling, divided

Directions
1. Combine the water and gelatin in a small saucepan set over medium-high heat. Stir constantly until gelatin fully dissolves.
2. In a medium mixing bowl, combine the lemon juice and condensed milk.
3. Add the gelatin mixture and stir to combine well.
4. Gently fold in the sour cream. Add 1¼ cups of the pie filling and mix well.
5. Transfer the filling to the crust. Refrigerate for 3-4 hours.
6. Top with the remaining pie filling and serve.

Nutrition (per serving)
Calories 211, fat 12 g, carbs 23 g, sugar 4 g,
Protein 3 g, sodium 124 mg

Cherry Pie

If you love cherries, this is the pie for you. It has cherry juice, cherries, and almond extract.

Serves 8 | Prep. time 25 minutes | Cooking time 1 hour

Ingredients
1¼ cups granulated sugar
⅓ cup corn starch
1 cup cherry juice
4 cups fresh tart cherries, pitted and thawed to room temperature
½ teaspoon ground cinnamon
¼ teaspoon ground nutmeg
¼ teaspoon almond extract

For the dough
2 cups all-purpose flour
½ teaspoon kosher salt
⅔ cup shortening
5-7 tablespoons ice-cold water
1 large egg, beaten (optional)

Directions

1. Preheat oven to 425°F (218°C).
2. In a large pot or saucepan, combine the sugar and cornstarch. Slowly add the cherry juice, stirring constantly, until smooth.
3. Bring to a boil, then stir constantly for 2 minutes, or until thickened. Remove the pot from the heat, then stir in the cherries, nutmeg, and almond extract. Set aside.
4. In a large mixing bowl, combine the flour, salt, and shortening until the mixture resembles coarse crumbles.

Gradually add the cold water and stir with a fork until a large ball of dough forms.
5. Make 2 balls out of the dough, one somewhat larger than the other.
6. On a lightly floured working surface, roll out the larger ball so it fits a (9-inch) pie plate. Place into a well-greased pie plate, trimming as necessary to fit the plate's edges (do not dispose of the trimmed dough).
7. Add the filling to the bottom crust.
8. Use the remaining dough to create a lattice crust. Cut, seal, and flute the edges, then place over the filling. If desired, use egg wash to brush over the dough.
9. Bake for 10 minutes, then lower the heat to 375°F (191°C) and bake for another 45-50 minutes.
10. Place the pie on a wire rack to cool, then serve.

Nutrition (per serving)
Calories 466, fat 17 g, carbs 73 g, sugar 41 g, Protein 5 g, sodium 161 mg

Impossible Cherry Pie

Cherries have never tasted this good with Impossible Cherry pie. It may not be the most popular of pies but with just one bite, this pie will surely gain a place in your heart and tastebuds.

Serves 8 | Prep time 15 minutes | Cooking time 35 minutes

Ingredients
For the pie
Olive oil cooking spray
½ cup Bisquick baking mix
¼ cup sugar
2 eggs
1 cup milk
2 tablespoons butter, softened
¼ teaspoon almond extract
21 ounces cherry pie filling

For the streusel
½ cup Bisquick baking mix
2 tablespoons cold butter
½ cup brown sugar
½ teaspoon ground cinnamon

Directions

1. Preheat the oven to 400°F (204°C).
2. Grease a 10x1½-inch pie dish with cooking spray.
3. For the pie, add the remaining ingredients except for cherry pie filling, and with a hand beater, beat until smooth.
4. Place the mixture into the prepared pie dish evenly.
5. Place the cherry pie filling on top evenly.
6. Bake for about 25 minutes.

7. Meanwhile, for the streusel, in a bowl, add the Bisquick baking mix, brown sugar, and cinnamon, and mix well.
8. With a pastry blender, cut in the butter until a crumbly mixture forms.
9. After 25 minutes of baking, remove the pie dish from the oven and top the pie with streusel.
10. Bake for about 10 minutes or until the streusel is golden brown.
11. Remove the pie dish from the oven and place it onto a wire rack to cool for at least 2 hours before serving.

Nutrition (per serving)
Calories 287, fat 9 g, carbs 46 g, sugar 18 g,
Protein 3 g, sodium 268 mg

Royal Cranberry Pie

This pie, first made in the 1940s, has bright citrus flavors with lemon zest and an orange-flavored pie shell.

Serves 10 | Prep. time 25 minutes | Cooking time 30 minutes

Ingredients
1½ cups all-purpose flour, sifted
¾ teaspoon kosher salt
½ cup shortening
1 tablespoon orange zest
5 tablespoons orange juice

For the filling
2 tablespoons all-purpose flour
2 cups granulated sugar
¼ teaspoon kosher salt
⅔ cup water
3 cups cranberries
2 tablespoons unsalted butter
1 cup raisins
1 tablespoon lemon zest

Directions

1. Preheat oven to 425°F (218°C). Combine the salt and sifted flour.
2. Add the shortening and orange zest with a pastry blender or two knives until the pieces have a sand-like texture.
3. Gradually the orange juice until the dough is moist enough to stick together.
4. Roll out ⅔ of the dough on a lightly floured surface.
5. Press the dough loosely into a well-greased (9-inch) pie dish. Trim, seal, and flute the edges.

6. To make the filling, in a saucepan, add the flour, sugar, salt, and water. Bring to a boil over medium-high heat.
7. Add the cranberries, raisins, and lemon zest. Cook for about 10 minutes, or until they start to pop.
8. Add the butter, then cool for a few minutes. Transfer the filling into the pie crust.
9. Roll out any extra dough from trimming the pie. If desired, you can use cookie cutters to make shapes. Arrange the dough shapes over the filling.
10. Bake for 20 minutes. Cool the pie on a wire rack before serving.

Nutrition (per serving)
Calories 368, fat 9 g, carbs 68 g, sugar 44 g,
Protein 3 g, sodium 169 mg

Old-Fashioned Gooseberry Pie

This old-fashioned gooseberry pie has fresh berries along with tapioca and butter.

Serves 8 | Prep. time 15 minutes | Cooking time 45-50 minutes

Ingredients
Pastry for a two-crust (9-inch) pie
3 cups fresh gooseberries, divided
1½ cups granulated sugar
3 tablespoons quick-cooking tapioca
¼ teaspoon kosher salt
2 tablespoons unsalted butter

Directions

1. Preheat oven to 400°F (204°C).
2. In a medium bowl, crush ½ cup of the gooseberries.
3. Add the sugar, tapioca, and salt. Mix until well-combined.
4. Add the remaining whole gooseberries and combine.
5. Transfer to a medium saucepan and cook, stirring constantly, over medium heat until thickened, about 5 minutes.
6. Place the pastry in a (9-inch) pie pan.
7. Transfer the filling to the pastry and dot the top of the pastry with the butter.
8. Arrange the top pastry crust over the filling.
9. Bake for 10 minutes, then lower the temperature to 350°F (177°C). Bake the pie for an additional 30 minutes, or until the crust is golden-brown.
10. Let the pie cool slightly, then serve.

Nutrition (per serving)
Calories 368, fat 9 g, carbs 74 g, sugar 56 g,

Protein 2 g, sodium 13 mg

Curly Slab Jam Pie

This versatile recipe was brought to America by Eastern Europe settlers and became popular in the 1950s. Feel free to adjust the recipe to your liking.

Serves 12 | Prep time: 15 minutes | Cooking time 25 minutes

Ingredients
1 cup granulated sugar
2 cups all-purpose flour
3 large eggs, room temperature
½ teaspoon baking powder
¾ cup unsalted butter
1 cup fruit jam
2 tablespoons powdered sugar

Directions

1. Preheat oven to 350°F (177°C). Grease a 9x13-inch baking dish with cooking spray or butter.
2. Melt the butter in a saucepan over medium heat.
3. In a large mixing bowl, combine the eggs and sugar until frothy.
4. Stir in the flour and baking powder until combined.
5. Add the melted butter and, using your hands, knead the mixture into a smooth dough.
6. Divide the dough into ⅔ and ⅓ sections and set it aside.
7. Roll out the ⅔ section of the dough to cover the bottom of the baking dish.
8. Top the crust with a layer of jam.
9. Grate the ⅓ section of the dough over the layer of jam, then top with the remaining jam.
10. Bake for about 25-30 minutes or until golden brown.
11. Sprinkle with the powdered sugar and serve.

Nutrition (per serving)
Calories 263, fat 13 g, carbs 34.1 g, sugar 18.1 g, Protein 3.8 g, sodium 100 mg

Mom's Strawberry Pie

If you want to make your mom happy and feel so loved during Mother's Day or even just any other day, this pie will surely bring a big smile to her face.

Serves 8 | Prep. time 20 minutes | Cooking time 5 minutes

Ingredients
1 (9-inch) shortcrust pie shell, prebaked
1 quart strawberries
1 cup sugar, sifted
3 tablespoons cornstarch, sifted
¾ cup water
1 teaspoon lemon juice

Directions

1. In a small pot, simmer 1 cup of strawberries in water for 3-4 minutes.
2. Add sugar and cornstarch and cook until the mixture thickens.
3. Add lemon juice and remove from heat.
4. Layer the uncooked strawberries on the pie crust then pour the strawberry glaze over the uncooked strawberries.

Nutrition (per serving)
Calories 227, fat 5 g, carbs 46 g, sugar 31 g,
Protein 2 g, sodium 87 mg

Easy Peasy No-Bake Strawberry Pie

Any pie topped with whipped cream is undeniably delicious and this easy-peasy strawberry pie is no exception. I discovered this pie recipe from my Mom's recipe box. It's one of her friends who made it often and wrote it down for her to keep. It's no doubt an easy peasy pie to make and everyone I served it to agreed that it's delicious

Serves 8 | Prep. time 40 minutes | Chill time 6 hours

Ingredients
1 (9-inch) shortcrust pie, prebaked
1 pint strawberries, sliced
2 tablespoons sugar
1 (15 ounces) can condensed milk
¼ cup lemon juice
Whipped cream, for topping

Directions

1. In a bowl, add strawberries and coat them with sugar. Leave for 30 minutes.
2. Add condensed milk and lemon juice.
3. Add the mixture over the pie crust.
4. Spread whipped cream over the berries.
5. Refrigerate for 6 hours.

Nutrition (per serving)
Calories 298, fat 11 g, carbs 48 g, sugar 36 g,
Protein 6 g, sodium 153 mg

Strawberry Sponge Pie

This traditional pie is filled with meringue and strawberries, making it light, crunchy, and spongelike.

Serves 8 | Prep. time 10 minutes | Cooking time 45 minutes

Ingredients
1 (9-inch) pie shell, baked and cooled
1 cup granulated sugar
2 tablespoons all-purpose flour
1 quart strawberries, hulled and sliced
2 large eggs, separated
½ cup whole milk

Directions

1. Preheat oven to 350°F (177°C). Refrigerate a (9-inch) pie plate on a cookie sheet in the fridge until needed.
2. Combine the strawberries, sugar, and flour in a large mixing bowl. Toss until the strawberries are well-coated.
3. In a small bowl, whisk together the milk and egg yolks until well combined.
4. Pour the egg mixture over the strawberries, then gently fold the mixture together until well-combined. Set aside.
5. Using a hand mixer, whip the egg whites in a medium mixing bowl until stiff peaks form.
6. Gently fold the stiffly beaten egg whites into the strawberry mixture until combined.
7. Transfer the strawberry filling into the prepared pie crust. Bake any remaining filling in ramekins along with the pie if you have any left over after filling the pie crust.
8. Bake for 45 minutes, or until the center is set.
9. Transfer the pie to a wire rack to cool. Top with whipped cream before serving.

Nutrition (per serving)
Calories 283, fat 9 g, carbs 48 g, sugar 32 g,
Protein 5 g, sodium 128 mg

Jell-O™ Strawberry Pie

Strawberry and Jell-o? It was all the rage in the 1970s. It seems like an unlikely pair, but this is such a fun and intense flavor combination and it's definitely so very easy to make.

Serves 6 | Prep. time 15 minutes | Chill time 4 hours+

Ingredients

1 (10-inch) pie crust, prebaked
3 tablespoons cornstarch
1 cup sugar
1 ½ cups water
1 (3 ounces) box strawberry Jell-O™
2 cups strawberries, sliced

Directions

1. In a saucepan over medium heat, mix cornstarch, sugar, and water. Once it boils, low the heat to a simmer and stir constantly until the mixture thickens.
2. Add the Jell-o and mix until completely dissolved.
3. Arrange the sliced strawberries at the bottom of the crust.
4. Slowly pour the gelatin mixture over the arranged strawberries.
5. Refrigerate for 4 hours or more until the pie has set.

Nutrition (per pie)

Calories 319, fat 17 g, carbs 42 g, sugar 17 g,
Protein 2 g, sodium 185 mg

Crumbled Strawberry Pie

Another strawberry pie variant, this crumble strawberry pie is not only prepared with sweet strawberry filling but also has a simple yet unforgettable crumb topping. My grandmother told me this way of making berry and other fruit pie was very popular in her youth, just before the war.

Serves 8 | Prep. time 15 minutes | Cooking time 1 hour

Ingredients
1 (9-inch) shortcrust pastry pie shell
Cinnamon sugar for dusting
Vanilla ice cream for serving

Crumbly topping
¾ cup white sugar
¾ cup all-purpose flour
6 tablespoons butter
1 pinch ground nutmeg
1 pinch ground cinnamon

Strawberries
4 cups fresh strawberries, hulled and rinsed
½ cup white sugar
½ cup all-purpose flour
1 tablespoon cornstarch

Directions
1. Preheat oven to 400°F (204°C).
2. To make the topping, in a bowl, combine sugar, flour, butter, cinnamon, and nutmeg. Mix until it becomes fluffy.

3. In another bowl, mix sugar, flour, and cornstarch. Slowly add the strawberries until all are coated with the mixture.
4. Add the coated strawberries to the middle of the pie crust. Cover them with the prepared topping.
5. Add about 15 pea-sized butter blobs over the topping.
6. Bake for 20 minutes.
7. Reduce heat to 375°F (191°C) then bake for 40 minutes more. Cover the pie crust edges with foil if it's starts to brown too much.
8. If desired, sprinkle a bit of cinnamon sugar over the pie's top when there are about 8-10 minutes left to bake.
9. Finish baking. Let cool on a wired rack and serve warm with vanilla ice cream f desired.

Nutrition (per serving)
Calories 410, fat 16 g, carbs 62 g, sugar 21 g,
Protein 4 g, sodium 179 mg

CITRUSY PIES

Lemon Cream Pie

This classic creamy lemon pie is made with lemon juice, lemon zest, sour cream, and whipped cream.

Serves 8 | Prep. time 10 minutes
Cooking time 20 minutes | Chill time 2 hours

Ingredients

1 (9-inch) pie shell, baked and cooled
1 cup granulated sugar
6 tablespoons corn-starch
1 cup whole milk
6 large egg yolks, lightly beaten
¼ cup salted butter
2 tablespoons lemon zest
½ cup freshly squeezed lemon juice
1 cup heavy whipping cream
½ cup sour cream

Directions

1. In a saucepan, add the sugar and corn starch. Mix until well-combined.
2. Add the milk and stir to combine. Cook while stirring for 8-12 minutes, or until bubbling and thickened, over medium heat.
3. Cook and stir on low heat for an additional 2 minutes, then turn off the heat.
4. Stir in a little of the hot filling into the bowl with the egg yolks. Then, transfer everything to the saucepan with the rest of the filling. Bring to a boil, then cook and stir for an additional 2 minutes.

5. Turn off the heat, then add the butter and lemon zest.
6. Add the lemon juice and stir to combine.
7. Wait 30 minutes to allow the filling to reach room temperature.
8. Beat the whipping cream in a chilled glass or metal mixing bowl until soft peaks form.
9. Gently combine the whipped cream, sour cream, and lemon filling by folding.
10. Transfer the entire mixture into the prepared pie shell. Refrigerate for at least 2 hours, then serve.

Nutrition (per serving)
Calories 481, fat 31 g, carbs 46 g, sugar 27 g,
Protein 5 g, sodium 201 mg

Lemon Meringue Pie

The origin of this pie dates back to the 1970s when this crisp-topped pie hit the food scene. It was a favorite among bakers who used it as a culinary means to impress their family and friends.

Serves 6–8 | Prep. time 10 minutes | Cooking time 50–55 minutes

Ingredients
Pastry
1⅜ cups flour
4 teaspoons superfine sugar
⅜ cup butter or margarine
Egg yolk

Filling
Zest and juice of 2 lemons
1½ tablespoons corn flour
1½ tablespoons butter
5 tablespoons superfine sugar
2 egg yolks

Meringue
2 egg whites
7 tablespoons superfine sugar

Directions

1. Mix the flour, butter, and sugar until you get a crumb-like consistency.
2. Add the egg yolk and enough water to mix until you get a firm dough.
3. Refrigerate for 20 minutes.
4. Preheat the oven to 400°F (204°C).

5. Add the prepared dough to an 8-inch flan tin and press it to cover the bottom surface.
6. Line with paper and add pastry weights (baking beans). Blind bake for about 15 minutes.
7. Remove the paper and weights. Bake for 5 minutes more until crispy.
8. Reduce temperature to 325°F (163°C).
9. In a bowl, combine the lemon juice and enough water to make around 10 ounces of liquid.
10. Combine 2 tablespoons of the lemon juice water with the corn flour in another bowl.
11. Add the corn flour mixture, lemon zest, sugar, and butter to a medium saucepan or skillet.
12. Heat over medium heat for 6–8 minutes, stirring continuously.
13. Remove from heat and let cool for a while.
14. Mix in the egg yolks and pour the mixture over the baked pastry.
15. In a mixing bowl, whisk the egg whites and sugar until the sugar dissolves.
16. Pour the meringue over the pastry filling and bake for 35–40 minutes until slightly golden and crisp.
17. Slice and serve warm.

Nutrition (per serving)
Calories 250, fat 13 g, carbs 31 g, sugar 14 g,
Protein 5 g, sodium 17 mg

Lemon Whey Pie

I found this recipe in my aunt Eunice recipes notes and was popular in the 1960s. It's made with fresh whey and topped with meringue.

Serves 4 | Prep. time 10 minutes | Cooking time 45 minutes

Ingredients
1 (9-inch) pie pastry shell, baked and cooled

For the filling
1½ cups fresh whey, divided
1 cup granulated sugar
3 ½ tablespoons arrowroot powder or organic corn starch
3 large egg yolks
1½ tablespoons unsalted butter, melted
½ teaspoon kosher salt
¼ cup lemon juice

For the meringue topping
3 large egg whites
¼ teaspoon cream of tartar
¼ teaspoon sea salt
½ teaspoon pure vanilla extract
6 tablespoons granulated sugar

Directions

1. Preheat oven to 350°F (177°C).
2. Bring 1 cup of whey to a roiling boil in a medium saucepan.
3. In the meantime, in a small mixing bowl, whisk to make a smooth paste with the sugar, arrowroot powder, and remaining ½ cup whey.

4. When the whey in the saucepan is boiling, add the paste and stir constantly until thickened.
5. In another small mixing bowl, gently whisk the butter, salt, and lemon juice together. To combine the egg yolks, slowly pour a small amount of the hot butter mixture into the egg yolk mixture while stirring. Repeat until all the eggs are incorporated.
6. Add the tempered mixture back to the saucepan and cook it for 2 more minutes, stirring constantly.
7. Transfer the mixture to the prepared pie shell. Set aside.
8. Now, start making the meringue. With an electric mixer, beat together the egg whites, cream of tartar, salt, and vanilla extract until foamy but not thickening.
9. Add the sugar 1 tablespoon at a time. Beat the mixture after each addition until you've added all the sugar. Make sure all the sugar has dissolved.
10. Continue beating the mixture at medium-high speed after all the sugar has been incorporated until stiff peaks form.
11. To prevent the meringue from deflating, place heaping spoonfuls of it around the pie's edges. Then, gently use the back of a spoon to seal it to the crust.
12. Make small "spikes" with the back of a spoon and add the remaining meringue to the center of the pie after creating the ring of meringue around the outside.
13. Bake the pie for 35 minutes.
14. Let the pie cool before serving.

Nutrition (per serving)
Calories 611, fat 21 g, carbs 105 g, sugar 83 g,
Protein 6 g, sodium 443 mg

No-Bake Whipped Angel Food Pie

This angel food pie, first invented in the 1960s, is light, fluffy, and lemony.

Serves 8 | Prep. time 30 minutes | Chill time 1-2 hours

Ingredients
1 (9-inch) pie shell, baked and cooled
1 (3-ounce) package lemon-flavored gelatin
½ cup granulated sugar
⅔ cup hot water
⅓ cup hot lemon juice
1 teaspoon lemon zest
1 cup evaporated milk
2 tablespoons lemon juice

Directions

1. Combine the gelatin, sugar, and hot lemon juice in a large mixing bowl with the hot lemon.
2. Chill the mixture until it has the texture of an unbeaten egg white.
3. Add the lemon zest.
4. Refrigerate the evaporated milk in a tray for 15-20 minutes, or until crystals form on the surface.
5. Whip the evaporated milk until very stiff peaks form.
6. Gently fold the whipped milk into the gelatin mixture. Transfer the filling into the baked crust.
7. Refrigerate for 1-2 hours or until set before serving.

Nutrition (per serving)
Calories 233, fat 5 g, carbs 43 g, sugar 29 g,
Protein 3 g, sodium 180 mg

Angel Pie

Angel pie dates back to the 1930s and the recipe has been passed down to the next generation. The pudding flavor can differ from cook to cook. My grandmother used to make it with lemons. And this is her recipe. If you like meringue, this will definitely be a hit in your family. You need to plan ahead for this pie as the filling should be refrigerated at least 8 hours before serving.

Serves 8 | Chill time 8 hours
Prep. time 15 minutes | Cooking time 8 minutes

Ingredients
For the meringue pie crust
Butter and flour for greasing and dusting
3 extra large egg whites
1 pinch cream of tartar
1 teaspoon pure vanilla extract
¾ cup white sugar

For the lemon filling
5 egg yolks
½ cup sugar
¼ cup lemon juice
Zest of 1 lemon

Whipped Cream Topping
1 cup heavy cream, chilled
2-4 tablespoons confectioner's sugar
1 teaspoon vanilla
Gelatin to stabilize cream (optional)
¼ tablespoon water

Directions
For the meringue pie crust

1. Preheat the oven to 275°F (135°C) and place the oven rack in the middle position.
2. Coat a 10-inch-deep pie pan with butter and lightly flour the pan. A glass pie pan such as Pyrex works best. Remove excess flour by reversing the pan over the sink.
3. In an electric stand mixer with the whisk attachment on, add the egg whites, vanilla, and a pinch of tartar. Beat on low speed until foamy.
4. Increase speed to high and gradually add the sugar. Beat until stiff peaks form.
5. Spread the meringue evenly into the pie dish with a spatula or the back of a wooden spoon.
6. Place into the oven and bake for 1 hour. Turn off the oven and let the meringue shell rest in the oven for 1 more hour. Make sure not to open the oven door as the meringue continues to dry up.
7. Remove from the oven and let cool completely.

For the lemon filling

8. While the pie shell is cooling down, prepare the filling.
9. Beat the yolks until they are thickened and heat them gently in a double boiler.
10. While continuously beating, add the sugar, lemon juice, and zest.
11. Continue cooking and stirring until the filling is lightly colored and thick.
12. Remove the mixture from the heat and let it cool completely.
13. Add the lemon filling to the meringue pie crust, cover with plastic wrap, and refrigerate for at least 8 hours and up to 12 hours.

For the topping

14. If you are using gelatin, heat the water and add the gelatin, stirring until it is completely dissolved.
15. Let the gelatin cool down a little, but don't let it set.
16. Whip the cream to soft peaks, and gradually add the sugar and vanilla while whipping.
17. Add the gelatin in a thin stream while whipping continuously.

To assemble

18. Take 1 cup of the whipped cream topping and gently fold it into the lemon filling.
19. Fill the meringue crust with the rest of the filling.
20. Spoon the remaining whipped cream topping over the filling, and chill.

Nutrition (per serving)
Calories 292, fat 15 g, carbs 37 g, sugar 34 g,
Protein 4 g, sodium 35 mg

Lemonade Chiffon Pie

This pie first arose in the 50s. It is made with a lemonade crust and tastes so good that you'll want to eat it straight out of the pie plate.

Serves 8 | Prep. time 15 minutes
Cooking time 5-10 minutes | Chill time 30 minutes

Ingredients
1 (9-inch) plain pastry pie shell, baked
1 envelope Knox gelatin, unflavored
½ cup cold water
⅛ teaspoon kosher salt
4 large eggs, separated
16 ounces frozen concentrated lemonade, thawed
½ cup granulated sugar
½ cup heavy cream, whipped
Chopped coconut, for garnish
6 medium strawberries, hulled and sliced

Directions

1. On top of a double boiler, sprinkle the gelatin.
2. Add the salt and egg yolks and mix until well combined.
3. Cook over boiling water, constantly stirring, until somewhat thickened and gelatin dissolves about 3 minutes.
4. Remove from the heat, then add the lemonade.
5. Stirring occasionally cools the mixture until it forms a small mound on a spoon.
6. Beat the egg whites with a hand mixer in a large mixing bowl. Beat until stiff peaks form.
7. Add the sugar slowly, beating thoroughly after each addition.
8. Add the gelatin mixture and combine well.

9. Gently fold in the whipped cream until combined.
10. Garnish with the chopped coconut, then transfer to the prepared pie shell.
11. Refrigerate until completely set, then serve.

Nutrition (per serving)
Calories 259, fat 13 g, carbs 32 g, sugar 23 g,
Protein 6 g, sodium 137 mg

Lemonade Icebox Pie

This American southern classic tastes like summer. The fresh, tart sweetness of the creamy pie with the crisp graham crust is a real treat for the taste buds!

Serves 8 | Prep. time 10 minutes

Ingredients

1 (9-inch) prepared graham cracker crust
8 ounces cream cheese, softened
1 (14-ounce) can sweetened condensed milk
¾ cup lemonade concentrate, thawed
½ teaspoon vanilla extract
Pinch salt
8 ounces frozen whipped topping, thawed
2 drops yellow food coloring, optional
Lemon slices (well drained) or zest for serving

Directions

1. In a mixing bowl, beat the cream cheese and sweetened condensed milk together until thoroughly combined.
2. Add the lemonade concentrate, vanilla, and salt. Mix well.
3. Fold in the whipped topping and food coloring, if using.
4. Spoon the pie filling into the crust and freeze until set.
5. Garnish with lemon slices or zest and serve.

Nutrition (per serving)

Calories 499, fat 24 g, carbs 63 g, sugar 48 g,
Protein 7 g, sodium 272 mg

Lime Cheesecake Pie

This lime cheesecake pie was first made in the 1950s. This recipe is so smooth and refreshing.

*Serves 8 | Prep. time 15 minutes | Cooking time 35 minutes
Chill time 2 hours 30 minutes*

Ingredients
9 ounces cream cheese, softened
2 tablespoons unsalted butter
⅓ cup unsalted butter, melted
½ cup granulated sugar
1 large egg
2 tablespoons all-purpose flour
½ cup whole milk
¼ cup lemon juice
2 tablespoons lime zest

Graham crust
1¼ cups graham crumbs
⅓ cup butter, melted
¼ cup sugar

Directions

1. Preheat the oven to 350°F (177°C).
2. To make the crust, in a medium mixing bowl, combine 1¼ cups of the crumbs with ⅓ cup melted butter and ¼ cup sugar, well. For the topping, set aside ¼ cup of the mixture.
3. In a well-greased 8-inch pie plate, press the remaining mixture into the bottom and sides.
4. Refrigerate until completely set, at least 30 minutes.

5. In a large bowl, beat the cream cheese and butter together. Stir in the sugar and egg until well-combined.
6. Add the milk and flour, then combine.
7. Add the lime juice and peel, then combine again.
8. Transfer the mixture into the prepared graham cracker pie shell.
9. Bake for 35 minutes. Before serving, refrigerate the pie until completely set, about 2 hours.

Nutrition (per serving)
Calories 303, fat 15 g, carbs 35 g, sugar 18 g, Protein 4 g, sodium 171 mg

COCONUT AND PINEAPPLE PIES
Pineapple Cream Pie

This pineapple cream pie recipe is rich, smooth as velvet, and will melt in your mouth. It tastes exactly like when I was growing up. My mom's favorite pie!

Serves 8 | Prep. time 10 minutes
Cooking time 10 minutes | Chill time 3 hours

Ingredients
1 (9-inch) plain pastry pie crust, baked and cooled
1 cup granulated sugar
3 tablespoons all-purpose flour
½ teaspoon kosher salt
1 cup whole milk
1 (15-ounce) can pineapple, crushed and drained
2 large egg yolks
3 tablespoons unsalted butter

Directions

1. Combine the sugar, flour, and salt in a saucepan heated over medium heat. Cook for 3-5 minutes, whisking constantly until the mixture thickens and starts bubbling. Then, turn off the heat.
2. Add the butter, egg yolks, and pineapple to the milk mixture.
3. Reheat the mixture for 3-5 more minutes over medium heat, until it starts to bubble.
4. Cook for an additional 2 minutes while constantly stirring, until it's hot and thickened.
5. Transfer the mixture into the prepared pie crust. Refrigerate for at least 3 hours, then serve.

Nutrition (per serving)
Calories 324, fat 13 g, carbs 47 g, sugar 34 g,
Protein 3 g, sodium 313 mg

Pineapple No-Bake Pie

This 1980s-era pie has fresh pineapple chunks and yogurt for a healthier flavor.

*Serves 8 | Prep. time 15 minutes
Chill time 4 hours 45 minutes*

Ingredients
1 (9-inch) graham cracker crust
6 ounces pineapple yogurt
3 ½ cups Cool Whip topping
½ cup pineapple, finely chopped

Directions

1. In a medium mixing bowl, gently combine pineapple yogurt and whipped topping.
2. Mix in the pineapple until well-combined.
3. Transfer the filling to the crust.
4. Freeze for 4 hours or until set. Before cutting, refrigerate for 45 minutes.
5. Top the pie with any desired garnishes before serving. Freeze any leftovers.

Nutrition (per serving)
Calories 303, fat 15 g, carbs 35 g, sugar 18 g,
Protein 4 g, sodium 171 mg

Millionaire Pie

This is a million-dollar pie recipe made with cream, fruit, nuts, and a graham-cracker crust.

Serves 12 | Prep. time 10 minutes
Freezing time 8 hours or overnight

Ingredients

1 (9-inch) graham cracker crust, premade
1 (20-ounce) can crushed pineapple in juice, drained
1 (14-ounce) can condensed milk, sweetened
¼ cup lemon juice
1 (8-ounce) container whipped topping, frozen and thawed
1 cup shredded coconut flakes, sweetened
½ cup chopped pecans
1 (8-ounce) whipped topping, optional
Maraschino cherries, optional

Directions

1. To prepare the pineapple, squeeze as much juice as you can from the pineapple pieces. You can use the back of a spoon to drain them in a fine mesh strainer. Set aside.
2. Whisk together the condensed milk and lemon juice in a medium mixing bowl until just slightly thickened.
3. Add the lemon juice and stir to combine. Gently fold in the whipped topping.
4. Add the pecans, shredded coconut, and crushed pineapple. Mix until well-combined.
5. Transfer the pie filling into the graham cracker crust.
6. Smooth the top of the pie, then put a plastic pie crust lid over the pie.
7. Freeze the pie overnight.

8. An hour before serving, spread the second container of whipped topping over the top of the pie.
9. If desired, top with the pecans and maraschino cherries before serving.

Nutrition (per serving)
Calories 388, fat 18 g, carbs 53 g, sugar 40 g,
Protein 6 g, sodium 190 mg

Frozen Tropical Pie

This pie, created in the 1970s, has banana, pineapple, rum, cream, lime, and a unique ingredient: mayonnaise.

Serves 10 | Prep. time 10 minutes
Chill time 3-4 hours

Ingredients
1 large banana, sliced
½ cup maraschino cherries, chopped
1 tablespoon lime juice
1 cup mayonnaise
1 cup heavy cream, whipped
1 cup crushed pineapple, drained
¼ cup powdered sugar
3 tablespoons light rum or ¼ teaspoon rum flavoring
1 teaspoon lime zest

Directions

1. In a large bowl, combine the lime juice with the sliced bananas.
2. Gently fold in the mayonnaise and whipped cream.
3. Fold in the heavy cream, crushed pineapple, powdered sugar, rum, and lime zest.
4. Transfer the filling to a (9-inch) pie plate.
5. Refrigerate the pie until thick and set for about 3-4 hours. If desired, top with sliced lemon, lime, and maraschino cherries before serving.

Nutrition (per serving)
Calories 238, fat 20 g, carbs 11 g, sugar 5 g,
Protein 0 g, sodium 133 mg

Sawdust Pie

If you haven't had a slice of sawdust pie before, you'll surely add this to your list of favorites. It's so rich and buttery, and the addition of pecans and desiccated coconut is just perfection.

Serves 8 | Prep. time 5 minutes | Cooking time 35 minutes

Ingredients
1 (9-inch) pie shell

For the filling
1½ cups desiccated coconut
1½ cups graham cracker crumbs
1½ cups pecans, chopped
1½ cups sugar
1 cup egg whites

Directions

1. Preheat the oven to 350°F (177°C).
2. In a bowl, mix the ingredients for the filling EXCEPT for the egg whites.
3. Beat the egg whites just until they are foamy and stir them into the coconut mixture.
4. Pour it into the pie shell.
5. Bake until set (about 35 minutes).

Nutrition (per serving)
Calories 486, fat 27 g, carbs 57 g, sugar 41 g,
Protein 7 g, sodium 180 mg

Coconut Pie

This is a most refreshing pie made with buttermilk custard, and coconut flakes.

Serves 16 | Prep. time 10 minutes | Cooking time 50 minutes

Ingredients
2 (9-inch) pie shells
5 large eggs
2 cups granulated sugar
¾ cup buttermilk
½ cup unsalted butter, melted
1 (10-ounce) package coconut flakes
1 teaspoon pure vanilla extract

Directions

1. Preheat the oven to 350°F (177°C).
2. In a large mixing bowl, whisk the sugar and eggs until well combined.
3. Add the melted butter and buttermilk and stir until well combined.
4. Add the coconut and vanilla extract and stir again to combine.
5. Divide the filling into the (9-inch) pie shells.
6. Bake the coconut pie for 45-50 minutes or until golden brown.
7. Let cool somewhat before serving.

Nutrition (per serving)
Calories 368, fat 19 g, carbs 45 g, sugar 32 g,
Protein 4 g, sodium 241.6 mg

Koko Nut Pie

Introduced in 1950, this pie has a golden top and a luscious filling.

Serves 8 | Prep. time 10 minutes | Cooking time 45 minutes

Ingredients
14½ ounces pie pastry
2 large eggs, beaten
½ cup granulated sugar
1½ cups corn syrup
½ teaspoon kosher salt
2 tablespoons unsalted butter
1 teaspoon lemon juice
1¼ cups shredded coconut

Directions

1. Preheat the oven to 400°F (204°C).
2. Roll the puff pastry until ⅛-inch thick.
3. Line a (9-inch) pie pan with parchment paper, then press the pastry into the pan, trimming the edges as needed.
4. In a large bowl, add and combine all the other pie ingredients.
5. Transfer the mixture to the pastry shell.
6. Bake for 15 minutes, then lower the heat to 350°F (177°C) and continue baking for 30 minutes.
7. Serve warm or cold.

Nutrition (per serving)
Calories 583, fat 19 g, carbs 107 g, sugar 96 g,
Protein 4 g, sodium 399 mg

OTHER FRUITY PIES

Apricot Icebox Pie

This recipe comes from an old, yellowed card in my Aunt Kristie's recipe box—I think it's from the 1970s. It's different and fresh, and you're going to love it.

Serves 8 | Prep. time 30 minutes | Cooking time 15 minutes

Ingredients

For the crust
48 vanilla wafers, crushed
½ cup margarine, melted

For the filling
1½ cups icing sugar
¾ cup margarine, melted
3 eggs, beaten
1½ cups heavy cream
¼ cup sugar
½ cup chopped pecans
2 (13-ounce) cans apricot halves

Directions

1. Crush the wafers and mix in the melted margarine. Press the base into a (9-inch) pie plate and chill until set.
2. In a medium saucepan, combine the icing sugar, margarine, and eggs. Cook over medium heat, stirring constantly until thickened. Set the pot aside and let it cool a little.
3. Drain the apricots and cut them into bitesize pieces.
4. In a separate bowl, whip the cream until it begins to thicken, and gradually incorporate the ¼ cup of sugar.

Beat until stiff peaks form. Fold in the apricots and pecans with a spatula.
5. To assemble the pie, place the cooked filling on the bottom, and top with the apricot whipped cream.
6. Chill one hour before serving.

Nutrition (per serving)
Calories 742, fat 55 g, carbs 61 g, sugar 49 g,
Protein 6 g, sodium 380 mg

Banana Rum Pie

This 1960s pie is festive with a pecan pie shell and the goodness of bananas with a hint of rum. You can omit the rum if you are baking for children.

Serves 8 | Prep. time 40 minutes
Cooking time 35 minutes | Chill time 3-4 hours

Ingredients
For the pie crust
3 tablespoons pecan, finely chopped
1 cup sifted flour
½ teaspoon salt
1 teaspoon sugar (optional, for sweet pies)
½ teaspoon baking powder (optional)
½ cup butter or shortening (1 stick)
2-3 tablespoons cold water
Egg white (optional), for glaze

For the banana filling
1 (3 ¼-ounce) packet vanilla pudding mix
1 tablespoon gelatin, unflavored
2 ¼ cups whole milk
1 (7.2-ounce) package fluffy white frosting mix
1½ teaspoons rum or rum flavoring
Dash of kosher salt
Dash of ground nutmeg
3 large bananas, divided
1 ounce semisweet chocolate
1 tablespoon unsalted butter

Directions
To make the pie crust

1. Sift the flour, salt, sugar, and baking powder into a large bowl. Mix in the pecans and stir to combine well.
2. Cut in the butter or shortening using a pastry blender or two knives or, if you are using butter, rub it into the flour with your thumb and forefinger to make half-walnut or pea-sized lumps. If you are using a food processor, pulse until the mixture has the texture of cornmeal and drizzle in the water while processing until the mixture can be formed into a ball.
3. Sprinkle the mixture with water a little at a time, tossing with a fork. Sprinkle any dry areas and continue mixing lightly until the dough holds together when pressed with the thumb and forefinger and can be formed into a ball. Cover with plastic wrap and chill for 30-60 minutes.
4. Roll it out on a floured surface to the required size (there should be a 1-inch overhang), to about ⅛-inch thickness for the bottom crust, and slightly thinner for the top crust. Work quickly, handling the dough lightly.
5. Being careful not to stretch the dough, fold the bottom crust in half and place it over the pie pan, then gently unfold it to line the pan. Press the dough carefully into place. Fold in the overhang and flute the edges with your thumb and forefinger, or use a fork to make depressions around the border.
6. Brush with egg white, if desired, and prick thoroughly with a fork. To prevent shrinkage, you may line the crust with wax paper and fill it with rice or beans or top it with another pan and let it rest for about 10 minutes in a cool place.
7. Prick the dough with a fork and bake the unfilled crust at 450°F (232°C) for 15 minutes, or until it is a delicate golden brown in color. Let cool completely.

To make the filling

1. In a medium saucepan, combine the pudding mix and gelatin to make the filling.
2. Prepare the pudding as directed on the packaging, adding the milk as instructed.
3. Cover the pudding's surface with wax paper, remove from the heat, and set aside.
4. In a large mixing bowl, make the fluffy white frosting per package instructions.
5. Add salt, nutmeg, and either rum or rum flavoring. Stir to combine.
6. Gently fold the pudding into the frosting.
7. Slice 1 banana and spread it into the pastry shell, then cover with half the filling.
8. Add the second sliced banana and cover with the remaining filling.
9. Refrigerate the pie for 3-4 hours.
10. Slice the remaining banana diagonally and spread it over the pie.
11. In a small saucepan, melt the butter and chocolate until well combined.
12. Drizzle the chocolate evenly over the pie and serve.

Nutrition (per serving)
Calories 270, fat 8 g, carbs 43 g, sugar 25 g,
Protein 7 g, sodium 347 mg

Banana Cream Pie

When the summer comes and the antique cars take to the roads again, I sometimes think about the lifestyle those people are remembering – the 1950s, and the days of sock hops and diners. This recipe hails from then, and it's just the sort of thing you might order in one of those classic diners.

Serves 6 | Chill time 6 hours
Prep. time 10 minutes | Cooking time 30 minutes

Ingredients

For the crust
1 ¼ cups all-purpose flour
¾ teaspoon salt
1 tablespoon sugar
½ cup butter, cold
2–4 tablespoons ice water

For the filling
1 cup sugar
⅓ cup cornstarch
1 teaspoon salt
3 cups whole milk
4 egg yolks, beaten
3 tablespoons butter
1 teaspoon vanilla extract
2–3 bananas, sliced

Topping
2–3 cups whipped cream, for topping

Directions

1. Make the crust. Preheat the oven to 375°F (191°C).

2. In a mixing bowl, combine the flour, salt, and sugar. Cut in the butter until none of the lumps are larger than a pea.
3. Add the ice water a tablespoon at a time, mixing lightly with a fork, until the pastry is moist enough to cling together when pressed into a ball.
4. Roll out the dough and arrange it on a (9-inch) pie plate. Trim and flute the edges and pierce the bottom with a fork.
5. Bake for 10–12 minutes, or until the crust is golden brown. Set it aside to cool
6. In a saucepan, prepare the filling. Mix the sugar, cornstarch, salt, and milk. Cook until it bubbles, stirring constantly.
7. Beat the egg yolks, and then stir in a small amount of the hot filling, whisking constantly, to temper the egg. Add a bit more and mix until smooth, and then add this back to the pot.
8. Bring the pot to a slow boil and stir for two minutes.
9. Add the butter and vanilla and refrigerate for 30 minutes.
10. Spoon half the pudding into the cooled crust, and cover with banana slices. Add the rest of the pudding, cover, and refrigerate until set, at least 6 hours.
11. Serve topped with whipped cream.

Nutrition (per serving)
Calories 303, fat 8.7 g, carbs 53 g, sugar 29.3 g,
Protein 5.4 g, sodium 87 mg

Cherry-Peach Pandowdy

Pandowdy was a popular dessert in the 1800s, and we think it's time for it to make a comeback. It's like a cross between a cobbler and a pie.

Serves 12 | Prep. time 30 minutes | Cooking time 30 minutes

Ingredients

For the crust
2 cups all-purpose flour
1 tablespoon sugar
½ teaspoon salt
¾ cup cold unsalted butter, chopped
¼ cup cold vegetable shortening
4–5 tablespoons ice water

For the filling
2 ½ pounds peaches, pitted, peeled, and sliced, about 8 medium peaches (or about 6 cups frozen sliced peaches, thawed and drained from excess juices)
1½ pounds fresh or frozen (thawed) cherries, pitted
1 cup sugar
6 tablespoons all-purpose flour
1 teaspoon lemon zest
2 tablespoons fresh lemon juice
½ teaspoon salt

Egg wash
1 egg yolk
1 tablespoon water

Directions

1. Combine the flour, salt, and sugar in a mixing bowl, and mix briefly until combined. Cut in the butter and shorten until the mixture has pea-sized pieces. Gradually drizzle in the water just until the dough comes together.
2. Knead the dough a few times and shape it into a small rectangle, wrap it, and refrigerate for 1 hour.
3. Preheat the oven to 400°F (204°C), and lightly coat an 11x8 baking or pie dish with butter.
4. Combine all the filling ingredients in a mixing bowl and pour them into the prepared pan.
5. Roll out the dough to a 12-inch square (it will be thick) and cut it into 16 pieces. Arrange the pieces over the filling, overlapping the edges.
6. Prepare the egg wash and brush it over the pastry.
7. Bake for 30 minutes, or until the filling is bubbly and the pastry is golden. Cover it with foil halfway through to prevent over-browning, if needed.

Nutrition (per serving)
Calories 354, fat 16 g, carbs 50 g, sugar 29 g,
Protein 4 g, sodium 100 mg

Peach Pie

This wonderful peach pie is made with fresh peaches, eggs, and butter. Its streusel topping sets this pie apart from other pies.

Serves 8 | Prep. time 25 minutes | Cooking time 40-45 minutes

Ingredients
1 (9-inch) plain pastry pie shell
1 large egg white, lightly beaten
6 cups fresh peaches, cored, sliced, and peeled
2 tablespoons plus ¾ cup all-purpose flour, divided
½ cup packed light brown sugar
⅓ cup granulated sugar
¼ cup cold butter, cubed

Directions

1. Preheat oven to 375°F (191°C).
2. On a lightly floured surface, roll out the dough into a circle that is ⅛-inch thick; transfer it to a (9-inch) pie plate.
3. Trim the crust at the rim and flute the edges.
4. Brush the egg white over the crust and refrigerate.
5. In the meantime, to make the filling, in a large mixing bowl, combine the peaches with 2 tablespoons of flour.
6. In a small mixing bowl, combine the remaining ¾ cup of flour, both sugars, and butter. Stir in the butter until the mixture resembles coarse sand.
7. Transfer ⅔ of the flour mixture to the crust, then top with the peach mixture. Add the remaining flour mixture to complete.
8. Bake for 40-45 minutes, or until the peaches are soft and the filling is bubbling.
9. For the final 15 minutes, cover the pie crust with foil if it starts to brown too quickly.

10. Let the pie cool slightly before serving.

Nutrition (per serving)
Calories 404, fat 18 g, carbs 58 g, sugar 32 g,
Protein 5 g, sodium 212 mg

Peach Parfait Pie

This is another traditional pie made with an almond-infused peach filling and an oat crust.

*Serves 8 | Prep. time 15 minutes
Cooking time 15 minutes | Chill time 3 hours*

Ingredients
<u>For the crust</u>
1 cup rolled oats
½ cup slivered almonds
½ cup light brown sugar
⅓ cup unsalted butter, melted

<u>Filling</u>
1 (25-ounce) package unflavored gelatin
¾ cup + 2 tablespoons orange juice, divided
1 pint vanilla ice cream
2 cups fresh peaches, diced
¼ teaspoon almond extract

Directions

1. Preheat oven to 325°F (163°C).
2. Spread out the oats on a well-greased cookie sheet.
3. Toast the oats for 5 minutes in the preheated oven.
4. After toasting the oats, add the almonds, and toast for an additional 5 minutes.
5. Remove from the oven, then transfer to a large mixing bowl.
6. Combine the oat mixture with the brown sugar and melted butter.
7. Pour the oats mixture into a (9-inch) pie pan. Press the mixture down to the bottom and sides of the pan. Transfer

to the refrigerator.
8. Add the orange juice to a large saucepan, bring to a boil, then turn off the heat. Using a whisk, slowly add the gelatin and stir until fully dissolved. Add the ice cream and combine until melted and the mixture is smooth.
9. Fold in the peaches and almond extract.
10. Fill the chilled pie crust with the peach filling.
11. Serve after refrigerating for at least 3 hours.

Nutrition (per serving)
Calories 289, fat 15 g, carbs 34 g, sugar 24 g,
Protein 4 g, sodium 89 mg

Old-Fashioned Pear Pie

We used to have a pear tree in our backyard when I was growing up and my dad could not wait until the pear were ripe for picking because he knew my mom would make her fabulous pear pie. She has made this recipe so often and would even double up the recipe and freeze it.

Serves 8 | Prep. time 30 minutes | Cooking time 3 hours

Ingredients
2 (9-inch) pie shells
3 tablespoons all-purpose flour
½ cup granulated sugar
¼ teaspoon salt
1 teaspoon ground cinnamon
½ teaspoon ground nutmeg
1 teaspoon lemon zest
A pinch of ground ginger
5 cups ripe pears, peeled, cored, and sliced half-inch pieces
2 tablespoons lemon juice
1 tablespoon cold butter, cut into 6 small pieces
1 egg mixed with 1 tablespoon cold water
White granulated sugar for dusting
Whipped cream or vanilla ice cream for serving

Directions

1. Preheat oven to 450°F (232°C). Grease a pie dish side with cooking spray or butter. Line the dish with the uncooked pie crust.
2. In a bowl, mix flour, sugar, salt, cinnamon, nutmeg, ground ginger, and lemon zest.

3. Add the sliced pears and coat them with the flour mixture.
4. Arrange the coated pears over the crust.
5. Add lemon juice over the remaining contents of the bowl and toss around until all remaining flour or sugar is picked up. Pour over the pears and add the pieces of butter over the pears.
6. Cover the filling with the remaining pie crust and tuck the edges to make a seam. Slice 4 slits to allow venting.
7. Brush the pie crust with egg wash and sugar, if desired.
8. Cover the edges of the pie crust with aluminum foil to prevent the edges from burning.
9. Bake for 10 minutes then reduce heat to 350°F (177°C) then bake for 40 minutes more until the pie is golden brown.
10. Remove the foil and let it cool for 3 hours.
11. Serve with whipped cream or vanilla ice cream.

Nutrition (per serving)
Calories 325, fat 13 g, carbs 51 g, sugar 4 g,
Protein 3 g, sodium 260 mg

Rhubarb Strawberry Pie

Have a bite of this sensational strawberry and rhubarb pie baked to perfection with a sweet and tart flavor. You'll love this as a springtime dessert especially when paired with vanilla ice cream.

Serves 8 | Prep. time 10 minutes | Cooking time 1 hour

Ingredients

2 (9-inch) plain pastry pie shells
2 cups rhubarb, chopped
2 cups sliced strawberries
1 ⅓ cups sugar
6 tablespoons flour, divided
1 tablespoon butter

Directions

1. Preheat the oven to 450°F (232°C) and prepare a pie pan with the bottom crust.
2. Sprinkle 2 tablespoons of the flour mixture over the bottom of the pie shell.
3. In a bowl, mix the rhubarb, strawberry, sugar, and remaining flour.
4. Spread the rhubarb-strawberry mixture in the pie shell.
5. Dot with butter. Cover with the second piece of pastry. Trim and flute the edges.
6. Make cuts on the top as vents.
7. Place the pie on the lowest rack and bake for 15 minutes. Reduce the temperature to 350°F (177°C) and bake 45 minutes longer.

Nutrition (per serving)

Calories 361, fat 12 g, carbs 65 g, sugar 38 g,
Protein 3 g, sodium 172 mg

Mom's Vintage Rhubarb Pie

This recipe dates back to the 1920s and always brings back golden memories of going to cut the rhubarb in our garden and eating a piece of the pie together with my mom as soon as it had cool down a bit. Sometimes, she would just do the regular crust and sometimes with a lattice pattern. I add coarse sugar on the top for added sweetness!

Serves 8 | Prep. time 10 minutes | Cooking time 50 minutes

Ingredients
1 (10-inch) double crust pie crust
2 tablespoons flour
2 eggs, beaten
3 cups rhubarb, chopped into ½-inch pieces
1 cup sugar
Egg wash (whisk 1 egg and 2 tablespoons of water)

Directions

1. Preheat the oven to 425°F (218°C). Grease a (9-inch) pie pan with melted butter or cooking spray.
2. Mix all the filling ingredients in a medium bowl. Combine well.
3. Arrange the bottom pie crust over the pie pan and spoon the filling mixture into it.
4. Place the top crust atop the filling and crimp the edges together with the bottom crust. Cut off the extra dough if needed
5. Cut some holes in the top crust for steam to escape. Brush some of the egg wash lightly on the crust top.
6. Bake for 15 minutes.
7. Turn down the temperature to 325°F (163°C) and bake for 30-45 minutes more, until the top is evenly golden.

8. Serve warm.

Note: For a lattice pattern, lay the top crust flat on a flour-dusted cutting and cut even strips of dough of ½ to ¾ -inch wide. I use a ruler and a pizza cutter for this step. Place half of the dough strips over the pie's rhubarb filling, in parallel lines, spaced evenly. From the middle, fold over every other strip to the same side. Lay a strip of dough perpendicular to the already placed strips to start your weaving pattern in the middle of the pie, at the fold. Fold the strips back down over the just placed strip. Fold the other strips that were not the first time over the strip that was just placed and lay another strip of dough at the fold. And continue in this fashion until all the pie is covered. Crimp the edges of the strip with the bottom crust.

Nutrition (per serving)
Calories 264, fat 9 g, carbs 43 g, sugar 26 g,
Protein 4 g, sodium 143 mg

Printed in Great Britain
by Amazon